H. Lloyd Goodall, Jr., Ph.D., is an associate professor in organizational communication at The University of Alabama in Huntsville. In addition to teaching and writing, he is also the private corporate communication consultant who was honored in 1983 by receiving the Jaycees Outstanding Young Educator and Toastmasters International Award for Communication Excellence.

Gerald M. Phillips, Ph.D., is a professor of speech communication at The Pennsylvania State University. In addition to teaching and writing more than twenty books on business and professional communication skills, he is director of the Program for Disturbed Communication at Penn State, and a private corporate communication consultant.

Making It
in any
Organization

H. Lloyd Goodall, Jr.
Gerald M. Phillips

A SPECTRUM BOOK

Prentice-Hall, Inc., Englewood Cliffs, N.J. 07632

Library of Congress Cataloging in Publication Data

GOODALL, H. LLOYD.
    Making it in any organization.

    "A Spectrum Book."
    1. Organizational behavior.   2. Interpersonal
communication.   I. Phillips, Gerald M.   II. Title.
HD58.7.G66 1984   650.1   84-13376
ISBN 0-13-547241-5
ISBN 0-13-547233-4 (pbk.)

© 1984 by Prentice-Hall, Inc., Englewood Cliffs, New Jersey 07632

A SPECTRUM BOOK

Manufacturing buyer: Doreen Cavallo
Cover design: Hal Siegel

ISBN 0-13-547233-4 {PBK.}

ISBN 0-13-547241-5

10 9 8 7 6 5 4 3 2 1

Printed in the United States of America

This book is available at a special discount when ordered
in bulk quantities. Contact Prentice-Hall, Inc., General
Publishing Division, Special Sales, Englewood Cliffs, N. J. 07632.

Prentice-Hall International, Inc., *London*
Prentice-Hall of Australia Pty. Limited, *Sydney*
Prentice-Hall Canada Inc., *Toronto*
Prentice-Hall of India Private Limited, *New Delhi*
Prentice-Hall of Japan, Inc., *Tokyo*
Prentice-Hall of Southeast Asia Pte. Ltd., *Singapore*
Whitehall Books Limited, *Wellington, New Zealand*
Editora Prentice-Hall do Brasil Ltda., *Rio de Janeiro*

CONTENTS

This book is respectfully dedicated to our readers, for whom, and because of whom, the book was written.

Once again our authorial efforts were warmly and generously supported by our immediate superiors, Donna and Nancy, for whom this expression of gratitude seems exceedingly insufficient and small.

PREFACE

This is a book about making it in America.

This is a book about *managing your performances* in the presence of others who can help you become healthy, wealthy, and wise. It is a book of practical advice based on years of scholarly research in a variety of academic disciplines, including administrative science, psychology, sociology, history, theatre, literature, and speech communication. We have translated research findings into simpler statements about what you can do to improve your chances of getting the responses you seek from others, especially those special others whose responses are very important to you.

We wrote the book for three reasons. First, we wanted to continue a tradition we started in an earlier volume entitled *Loving and Living: Improve Your Friendships and Marriage* (Prentice-Hall/ Spectrum Books, 1983). This tradition is to provide practical understandings of subjects of interest to almost everyone, subjects about which much has been written in academic journals and books, but about which very little knowledge finds its way to popular audiences. The second was to make more money. As practicing academics, both authors suffer from the lack of fiscal respect currently shown to college professors by state and federal governments. By writing a book like this one, we stand a chance of withstanding inflation. Third, we wanted to address the idea of succeeding in American organizations from a pragmatic perspective. We feel that too many books offer the wrong kinds of advisories about how to win friends and influence the people we work with and for, books either ignorant of the research or just plain defiant about one particular way of doing it better, often to the exclusion of other good ways. Our book is a collection of various ways and means of making it in American organizations, a guidebook to choices only you can ultimately make.

What do we mean by the awesome phrase "making it"? We do *not* mean getting ahead at unnecessary cost to others or to your health. We do *not* mean succeeding for its own sake. We do *not* mean, to borrow a title from another book with a similar aim, "Looking Out For Number 1." We do *not* promise you will rise to the top of the corporate cream, nor do we guarantee you will become a better person by reading these chapters. We define "making it" by asking you to define *what you seek from others*. This is not a a cop-out. It is a difficult question to answer. For instance, you might define "making it" by the following general goals:

> Getting the job in the company I want to work for;
>
> Doing the job well enough to merit increases in pay, kind words from others I work with, and stability in my own life;
>
> Having the opportunity to advance my career when I want to, rather than when my superiors think I should;
>
> Feeling confident about my professional skills and knowledge;
>
> Feeling confident in social settings because I can talk about a wide range of topics both related and unrelated to my work;
>
> Believing that what I do for a living counts in the world, that my labor is worth more than just a paycheck;
>
> Knowing that others care about me not just because of what I can do for them, but because of who and what I am, what I stand for, and what I represent to them.

These are truly admirable goals. However, they may not be *your* goals. To understand what "making it" means to you, you need to begin by defining *how you would know if you made it*.

The second term requiring definition is "organization." We claim to address the subject of "Making It in any Organization." By "organization" we mean any business, agency, commercial enterprise operated for profit, industry, nonprofit group, company, or government program that can be identified by the following characteristics:

1. It deals with a good, service, product, or process that is planned, designed, manufactured, stored, delivered, or otherwise dealt with by people.
2. It has a hierarchy of organization and control (e.g., including a head of operations, CEO, manager, or boss, and some group of workers).
3. It operates under the constraints of time and money.
4. It offers opportunities for work and advancement.

So much for the meaning of the title of our book. We are concerned with helping you define and reach specific goals strategically designed to help you make it in any organization.

chapter one

INTRODUCING THE PERFORMANCE PERSONALITY

"We know what we are, but know not what we may be."
—WILLIAM SHAKESPEARE

"Work is the only source of dignity."
—F. SCOTT FITZGERALD

THE MEANINGS OF ORGANIZATIONAL AMERICA

The organizations of America are clearly the masters of us all. According to recent statistics, nearly four million new jobs are created annually in these United States.[1] All of these jobs are created in, by, or for organizations, corporations, and government agencies.

For most persons, organizational life begins at birth and continues relatively uninterrupted (barring a depression) until death. We are born in hospitals, reared in homes financed by banks or mortgage companies, driven to kindergarden in automobiles manufactured by industries, schooled in mismanaged bureaucracies

[1]D. Yankelovich, *The New Rules* (New York: Random House, 1981), p. 167–168.

that somehow advance most of us through elementary, middle, secondary, higher, and continuing educations, work in organizations and agencies, pay utility bills, and so forth until death parts us from secular concerns and the Great Spirit in the sky assigns us to eternity in one of the ultimate bureaucracies named by Dante as the circles of hell, limbo, or heaven.

By the time most of us are ready to enter careers we have chosen, we are more familiar with languages of corporate organization than we are with the languages of our bodies and selves. We may not understand the complexities of the world economy any more clearly than we understand triple by-pass surgery, but we are partners in both process's evolution and, potentially, their demise. We may not comprehend the meaning of our behavior, of the bills we pay or the buttons we push, but we complete them in a rhythm of fascinating precision. While we marvel at the amazing organization of ants, and make bad jokes about their compulsion to specialize, we are oblivious to our own commitment to organization and specialization. While we claim self-reliance and independence as co-equal states of virtue, we more often than not succumb to dependence on organizations and ignorance of the technologies that run them and us. The question is as it always has been, "Which is to be the master . . . that's all." But in an age in which the guiding metaphor is drawn from systems theory, the answer is fuzzy and purely academic because all inputs and outcomes are interdependent. Perhaps for these reasons, for the sake of the complexities and subtleties of organizational living, we tend to think of our work in vague terms and of ourselves in precise ones.

Like the world view prior to Copernicus, we cling to the notion that we are the centers of the universe, and organizational life evolves and revolves around us. In our own time, our collective search for self-fulfillment and pleasure has so superseded our commitment to working and making ends meet as to redefine our goals. No longer are many of us content to work for a living, to provide economic security for our families, or simply to advance our careers in service to the firm; instead we demand need fulfillment, gratification on the job, meaningful relations with coworkers and superiors, and whatever else we mean when we utter the wholly abstract phrase "job satisfaction." We advance our careers because advancement feels good. We want to become successful because not to become successful is supposed to feel bad. We think less of service to the firm employing us, and more and more about service to ourselves. The reason for choosing a career is to make money, lots of money, and the purpose of working is to enjoy what you are doing and those with whom you do it. Life is too short, after all.

One major problem resulting from this personalized view of work is the lack of opportunities for advancement and the absence of room at the top. Computer technology in office automation makes it possible to remove whole levels of middle management from organizational charts as access to information and simulated decision models replaces the need for human management. With more college graduates seeking work in American organizations, and more and more post-graduate degrees being granted each year, and with more demands being made for symbols and status of success, we seem to be running out of corporate room. Whereas our parents may have defined success as moving from blue collar to white collar positions within the same organization, our generation begins with white collar work and seeks nothing less than a vice-presidency before 40, regardless of where we have to go to get it. Many organizations are already so topheavy in the executive ranks as to make their organizational charts resemble inverted pears.

This may seem to be a bleak portrait for a book about making it in American organizations. However, we feel it is a realistic portrait, and to adequately plan a successful career these days requires a strong dose of realism. The point here is we do live in a technologically informed, organizational nation, a place where change is rapid and computers are supreme. To do well will become increasingly difficult. We will have to know more about how organizations operate, how decisions are made, how groups work, how computers function, how to relate with peers, superiors, and subordinates, and how to get the responses you seek from others. In short, you will have to learn how to develop what we call "the performance personality." In the next section, we discuss the performance personality by contrasting it to older traits associated with organizational advancement.

THE MYTH OF THE GIFTED: BORN TO BE GREAT RECONSIDERED

Some people have all the advantages. There are those persons who do possess family wealth and connections, awesome personal beauty, intelligence, and a sense of humor. There are these people walking around among us who somehow survive these traits to rise to prominence in America. We say "survive" these traits because it is often more difficult for persons who have inherited both genetic and financial propensities for success to actually succeed. It is too easy to loaf around the mansion sipping champagne, admiring the one you love in mirrors.

Of course there are those persons who do succeed because of wealth, family connections, or personal beauty and wit. However, they seldom succeed for very long. They may graduate from prestigious schools (although with a "C−" average) and assume an important position with Dad's firm (at Mommy's insistence), but by the time the first or second appraisal review occurs, they may well have shown what bumbling bimbos they really are. For example, from a circle of 11 well-to-do friends of one of the author's childhoods, all of whom had the blue planet by its spinning nexus from birth, only one of them has yet to amount to anything. Most of the others, after brief stints at family-controlled corporations, have had to retreat to the family, or to artist's colonies, or have gone into the medical supply field. Two are dead from drug overdoses, and one is regularly hospitalized.

There is a dangerous myth of the gifted pervading American beliefs about what it *really* takes to succeed. The term "gifted" implies some mysterious something, out of some even more mysterious somewhere, was somehow bestowed on the individual. It is as if she or he was blessed by some divine personage, touched by the infinite wisdom of the ages. We read about "gifted" children, those small citizens who surpass normal expectations on an intelligence test. We applaud the efforts of their usually common parents who suddenly give in to the possible presence of genius and stock the family den with a library of classics and the gifted child's bedroom with a home computer. Fortunately, we live in an age that

4

values intelligence, and encourages the efforts of those blessed with the skill or insight to do well on intelligence tests. In other cultures, at other times, these "gifted" children would stand equal chances of being slaughtered because they were clearly "abnormal," or revered as messengers from the gods.

The controversy concerning what exactly intelligence tests measure is problematic.[2] The work of early pioneers has been debunked by both critics and scientists. Evidence suggests the "gift" of being "gifted" may only be the ability to perform well on a test desperately in need of that kind of validation. Whatever intelligence is, we tend to reward "it" when "it" meets whatever criteria we establish for "it." For example, in the famous educational psychology experiment of the 1960s, experts discovered that if a teacher was told a pupil was "bright," the teacher treated the pupil as one would treat a bright person, thus increasing the pupil's self-esteem and the frequency of opportunities to prove the original judgment correct. Conversely, if the teacher was told the child was dumb as stone, chances were the pupil proved herself or himself to be dumb as stone, at least insofar as the teacher's judgments were concerned.

The seemingly unsolvable problem of measuring intelligence does seem to suggest one important conclusion: *If someone in authority pronounces you intelligent, changes are good others will begin to treat you as a smart person.* So the real "gift" of the gifted may be the ability to know how to get someone in a position of authority to pronounce the magical word "intelligence" above their heads. The larger lesson is an entirely practical one, and it was first stated by the great American philosopher and social scientist George Herbert Mead.[3] Mead believed our identities were formed by the responses other persons made to us and about us. Hence, if we can influence how others learn to respond to us, then chances are we can define, or redefine, our identities.

The key to success on this planet is getting others to accept

[2]See S. J. Gould, *The Mismeasure of Man* (New York: W.W. Norton, 1981).
[3]See G. H. Mead, *Mind, Self, and Society*. (Chicago: University of Chicago Press, 1934).

what you claim to be. And the mysterious mechanism for turning that all-important key is not a "gift" bestowed by an intelligence test, but instead your own skill at gaining the responses you seek from others.

Americans are *born to be great*!

Now what red-blooded American citizen would disagree with that statement? Despite its biased flattery, recent evidence suggests we ought to take a more critical stand about our own destiny. Frances FitzGerald studied the evolution of American history textbooks in the decades of the twentieth century and discovered our American vision of history left out a lot of facts.[4] For a whole generation of Americans growing up in the 1940s through the 1960s who learned about "manifest destiny" in our country's expansion from sea to shining sea, the facts surrounding the corrupt politics of those decisions were carefully edited. This history we read, beyond this simple example, was a history of Americans as secular gods, of a race created in God's image and set upon the shores of Massachusetts Bay to establish the new Eden. Our wars were Holy Wars, our victories in them inevitable, our supremacy assured.

Vietnam veterans can testify to the impact some of those history lessons had on them in later life. Although we now have a national monument to the Vietnam War and those who died in it, the monument was paid for by the veterans themselves, and is at best a very solemn tribute to the myth of American history. For this generation, who grew up on a simple, powerful view of America's place in the world, the complexities of the 1960s and particularly of the Vietnam War could not be captured in the favorite bumper-sticker of the era: "America Right or Wrong: Love It or Leave It." The easy dichotomy of good guys and bad guys didn't leave any room for ambiguity or failure. Americans, by God, were not supposed to lose a war. But we did, and our myth of supremacy among the races of man, our divine infallibility, was tarnished.

During the mid-1970s we began to fight another war. Again,

[4]F. Fitzgerald, *America Revised* (New York: Vintage, 1979).

the war was, and still is, a struggle between "our" ways and "their" ways, and it is fought on the corporate conference tables of the world. The first shot was fired by the Arabs during the oil embargoes, shortages, and cartels. The second blast came with the wave of Japanese automobile and light truck sales, which pounded our harbors with cheaper, fuel-efficient, quality products at a time when GM, Ford, and Chrysler were still building hogs and dogs. Then, in the late 1970s and early 1980s the new Japanese management theories, popularly known as "Theory Z," challenged our assumptions about running businesses and strategic planning.[5] Where we had advocated centralized authority and independence, the Japanese management theories demonstrated the benefits of group decision making and interdependence. Where we advocated motivation-based theories of management, they demonstrated the utility of job satisfaction and family security as prime movers of women and men in organizations. And where we advocated the freedom to change jobs to improve our earning power and status, they demonstrated the necessity of keeping workers happy over the years and publicly discriminating against those who sought to terminate their employment for possible financial gains elsewhere.

Could Americans have been so wrong? The question we collectively asked ourselves may not be answerable, but asking it can be productive. Of course there are those who maintain "their" ways only work in Japan because of cultural values needed to suppress individuality. And there are those persons who mindlessly seek to imitate the ways of the Japanese to instantly improve the productivity and quality of products manufactured here. But neither the rejection or acceptance of the Japanese management styles is likely to get at the heart of the question. The question does not ask for consensus about the methods of the Japanese, but their ability to use them so successfully *against us*. Again, our myth of natural supremacy has been challenged, not just our way of doing business or managing people.

Everyone wants to be "King of the Hill." Everyone wants to be the "best" at something. In America, we have been reared to

---

[5]W. Ouchi, *Theory Z*. (Reading, Massachusetts: Addison-Wesley, 1980).

believe we *are* the best at everything, the king of all hills, however defined. In this respect, we resemble all the great cultures of history, from the ancient Egyptians to the wise Greeks to the decadent Romans, through all the kings and queens of England, the monarchs of the proud Germanic and Chinese empires, to the noble Sioux and Cherokee of our own native soil. We have, as Walt Whitman put it, "celebrated" ourselves. We have sung songs of our conquests and risen to the heights from which all others appear smaller, less potent, less capable.

Our view of ourselves as a nation may be a prime cause of our individual drives to succeed. However, it is not the *drive* to succeed that spells success, but the *ability to perform* successfully that marks the successful person. After all, you can want to be a genius, but unless others are willing to respond to you as a genius, to view your performances as worthy of praise, then your ambition probably will not be rewarded. It is ability and not blind ambition (thank you John Dean) that characterizes those persons who achieve greatness. Wealth, family connections, beauty, and intelligence can help, but the bottom line will always be *performance*.

The question becomes: How can I learn to perform successfully?

A Contemporary Intelligence Quiz

1. What was the name of the first computer? When was it invented? Who was the woman responsible for coining the term "bug" when referring to problems executing a computer program, and for what other term is she best known?
2. What was the name of the founder of IBM? Name three principles of his style of management. How do these compare with the principles of Japanese management? How could this possibly be?
3. Who invented the standard intelligence tests given to American school children? What is the statistical principle involved in validating the results of it? What is the theoretical flaw of this statistical principle when used to validate human intelligence?
4. In office settings, we find ourselves casually commenting on the meaning of someone else's behavior. Since we all see essentially the same behaviors, why is it we often have trouble agreeing on their meanings? Why is it that to answer this question you have to be able to first agree on the meaning of meaning or on the meaning of behavior?

If the previous questions intrigued you and were fun to answer, you should consider a career in academia. They aren't the kinds of questions you need to answer to make it in any other kind of organization. However, the following two questions should provide you with a basic test of your potential for the *performance personality*:

1. How hungry for success do you need to be to succeed? (Hint: The right answer begins "As hungry as I am right now because I am willing to do whatever it takes to make it.")
2. Can successful organizational behavior be learned? (Hint: Of course it can!! Why else would you be reading this book?)

THE PERFORMANCE PERSONALITY

The performance personality depends on three assumptions about what it takes to succeed on the job and with others:

1. The will to succeed;
2. The ability to adapt communication to the needs and expectations of others and situations; and
3. The ability to learn from past experiences and to set precise, do-able goals for the near and distant future.

The Will to Succeed

Of all the mysteries that have been explained by the sciences, of all the miracles of the human psyche and spirit revealed by psychologists, psychiatrists, poets, playwrights, rabbis and priests, the nature of *human will* remains both a mystery and a miracle.

What we call "will" does not reside in any internal organ, nor does it appear to be shaped or controlled by external or environmental influences. What we call "will" sums up our commonly felt urgency to name a powerful something that most of us feel ought to be called something. "Will" does nicely.

The philosopher Nietzsche believed the will was responsible for all human actions and emotions, and to direct the will was a godlike urge which, if used properly, could allow a person to overcome illness, mental fatigue, loss of sexual prowess, and even problems with other persons. The psychiatrist Leslie Farber admits to a determination to understand the will, and human uses of willing, and the study of what constitutes (and disrupts) the will is a focal point of his discipline.[6] In one essay, he describes the "two realms of will"—the unconscious, or general direction and directiveness we feel in all human activities (e.g., to win a game of tennis, to move up the corporate ladder, to alleviate an anxiety, etc.), and the conscious, or the urgent intentionality we call into being in specific situations or circumstances (e.g., changing the topspin of our tennis serve, influencing the boss to obtain a raise, reducing stress at moments of decision, etc.). These two realms of will are always in a kind of tormented dialogue with each other, a feverish exchange of controls and influences and acts of willing. Like two brothers who are very close and yet very different, their arguments can become volatile without becoming violent because that which binds them together as kin prevents them from destroying each other.

Farber goes on to argue that the opposite of will is *anxiety*, and "the consequences of willing what cannot be willed is that we fall into the distress we call anxiety."[7] In other words, we can wish, hope, dream, and even strain toward that which we define as desirable, but if we cannot obtain it, if we cannot hold it within our grasp and call it our own, our achievement, our success, our urgency turns against us and becomes the desperate feelings of anxiousness and inadequacy that can combine to destroy us. Hence, the will to succeed has the unique equipotential to both motivate our choices of actions, and to motivate the choice for self-destruction, which occurs when our choices of action fail to help us realize our goals.

The concept of will is bound necessarily to another concept, the concept of *self-presence*, or what we call "the performance personality." Simply put, the desire to succeed must be accompanied by the will to perform those actions that would define you as successful. The will to succeed depends on the ability to direct your actions and activities toward specific goals, to see your actions and especially your interactions with others as *meaningful performances*.

---

[6]L. Farber, *Lying, Despair, Jealousy, Envy, Sex, Suicide, Drugs, and the Good Life*. (New York: Harper Colophon, 1976), pp. 3–34.
[7]Farber, p. 7.

Adaptive Communication Practices

Any meaningful performance depends on effective and efficient communication. The term "communication" is as broadly used as it is misunderstood. For some authorities working from a humanistic psychology perspective indebted to such figures as Carl Rogers, Abraham Maslow, or Gregory Bateson, the function of communication is to validate experiences, authenticate personal and professional identities, and to provide mechanisms for inclusion, affection, and control in social situations. From this perspective, communication practices should be open, honest, spontaneous, and responsive to personal needs and goals. In the true spirit of the first and fifth amendments to our Constitution, speech should not only be exercised as a right and a freedom of expression, it should also be *expressive* in nature—that is, speech should be virtually uncontrolled.

In contrast to the humanistic psychology perspective are researchers in the *pragmatic* tradition sparked by the work of such pioneers as John Dewey, Charles Pierce, and William James. The work spawned by these generous minds indicates the function of speech is to gain appropriate and desirable responses from others, to reach definable goals, and to unite couples and groups in co-equal pursuits of happiness and well-being. The pragmatists present a radically different notion about what communication practices should be. Rather than encouraging spontaneous speech, uncontrolled, honest expressions of self, or total openness in relationships, the pragmatists encourage *controlled, rhetorical, adaptive* strategies for effective and efficient communication.

By *controlled* we mean you make active choices about the words you speak and actions you will perform based on (a) the likely outcomes of those choices, and (b) the desired results you hope to attain by performing those actions. You don't just "say whatever pops into your head," instead, you choose what you will say and do based on the goals you have for the situation.

By *rhetorical*, we mean communication is inherently persuasive, influential, and capable of inducing cooperation between or among persons. Here again you can make productive choices about what to say and do, and how to say and do it, which influence the likely outcomes of talk. You don't "just express yourself," instead, you try to understand what those expressions of self are likely to do to your listener. From the great rhetorical tradition, communication is viewed as an instrument equally capable of uniting and dividing persons. The objective of learning how to behave rhetorically is to improve your skill at prescribing goals for talk and working cooperatively with others to obtain them.

And by *adaptive*, we mean any communication should be listener- or audience-centered, it should be adapted to the needs and expectations of its receivers and the situation in which it occurs. Rather than "talking about myself, for my own reasons," the adaptive communicator strives to select from the available topics for talk those that include audience consideration, and those that are most likely to promote cooperation in obtaining goals.[8]

A popular, if somewhat dated adage has it that "you are what you eat." While there is certain truth to this statement, we believe regardless of what you choose to eat, *you are what you communicate*. Our identities are shaped by the responses we receive from others to our communication, and our ability to gain appropriate and desirable responses from others at home, at work, and out and about in society depend on our skill at adapting our choices of the words we speak, and the actions we perform, to the needs and expectations of our listeners and audiences.

Using Past Experiences to Establish Realistic Goals

A great American educator by the name of Wendell Johnson explained how and why many persons in the world of business and industry end up living lives of quiet desperation.[9] He defined the

---

[8]Research consistently demonstrates the advantages of what we call the adaptive approach to communicating. J. T. Wood, in her essay "Leading in Purposive Discussions: A Study in Adaptive Behavior," *Communication Monographs*, 44 (1977), 152–165, used this approach to reveal the essential skills of leadership relevant to organizational activities. H. L. Goodall, Jr., "Organizational Communication Competency: Using an Industrial Simulation to Teach Adaptive Skills," *Communication Quarterly*, 30 (1982), 182–195, demonstrated the relationship between the adaptive approach and organizational communication competencies. G. M. Phillips, *Help for Shy People* (Englewood Cliffs, N.J.: Prentice-Hall, 1981), showed how the adaptive approach could be used to help persons overcome shyness, particularly the kinds of anxieties that prevent persons from advancing their careers in organizations.

[9]W. Johnson, *People in Quandries*. (San Francisco: International Institute for General Semantics, 1948).

problem known as the IFD Syndrome (I = Idealization; F = Frustration; D = Demoralization). Here is an example of how this syndrome develops:

In childhood we learn that others, especially parents and peers, respond positively to expressions of our great expectations. At the ripe old age of 8, we learn to state confidently we intend to become lawyers, doctors, statespersons, or famous writers. After we have repeated these statements often enough over a period of years, these important others naturally come to expect us to try to live up to them. Parents sacrifice to send us to the "best schools," and to offer us the advantages they claim they never had. For the few who attain success in school, and who do enter organizational life with impeccable credentials, the world appears to have a very bright promise indeed. The goal then may become more precise—rising on the corporate ladder to the level of vice-president or CEO, usually by the age of 40.

Of course even fewer of the original aspirants for these positions actually make it, thus causing frustration among those who don't. Then, for those who don't make it to their idealized goals as fast or as successfully as they hoped to, the tendency is to behave much as the old Avis car rental commercials—*to try harder*. Unfortunately, "trying harder" doesn't mean much unless it is accompanied by the ability to learn from past experiences, and to develop the skills necessary for advancement. Then, for those in earnest pursuit of the American Dream, when advancement doesn't come, doesn't happen despite their harder efforts, frustration turns into demoralization—the belief that failure occurred because of corporate inequity or personal deficiencies. Instead of seeking professional help, or making productive uses of our past experiences to define new, attainable goals, we tend instead to seek escapes—alcohol, drugs, abandonment of families and friends, despair marked by envy and bitterness. Defining ourselves as failures in our professional aspirations, we tend to complete the scenario by failing also at home and in society. Or at least *believing* we have failed.

The odd fact about those of us for whom the previous description may be all too real is that we define ourselves as failures when by any realistic standard we have succeeded! We maintain responsible jobs, we contribute to our professions and our nation's economy, we have induced others to care about us. Yet we maintain we have failed, utterly, miserably, and end up succumbing to the general *ennui* by blaming ourselves, the victims of our own unrealized expectations spelled out in an eight-year old's breath. As Wendell Johnson demonstrated, the problem is not so much "us," as it is our inability to establish realistic goals and to learn from past mistakes.

These three assumptions establish the basis for understanding the governing attitude, the right frame of mind, out of which to develop your performance personality. These three ideas consistently will guide the advisories provided in this book. Embrace them and you have the basis to develop your own power of will, adaptive sensitivities, and pragmatic, realistic goals to guide your choices of succeeding in a world of diminishing opportunities.

chapter two

THE PERFORMANCE PERSONALITY SEIZES THE DAY

"A resume does not represent reality, it orders and describes it with a purpose in mind."

—EMPLOYMENT COUNSELOR

"You never get a second chance to make a good first impression."

—ANONYMOUS

PERSONAL EXPECTATIONS AND ORGANIZATIONAL REALITIES

You sit alone in one white corner of the outer office.

The secretary, who looked at you as if you had very little reason to continue breathing, said your interview was being delayed due to a "special meeting." You are to wait. You are supposed to "make yourself comfortable" on a cheap plastic straightback chair and "read a magazine or something until it is time." Her words ring like playful tears in your ears as you just sit there. *Fortune*, last week's *Time*, and a few odd copies of *Sales & Management* stare at you like broken promises. The building is too warm and you are uncomfortable in your suit.

15

Suddenly, you are called in to the office. The boss, your interviewer, is a short, squat, square-looking, slightly nervous and balding creature. She wears mauve lipstick badly and dark green eye makeup to mask the bags. She is apparently a chain-smoker. She flips through your application and résumé as if looking for misspelled words or decoding a secret message. She finally grunts, thumps the folder closed, and looks as if she just digested something that did not at all agree with her. She is obviously impatient as the interview begins. . . .

What you have just read can and does happen.

It happens to those persons who dream the American Dream of making it big in organizations, and who pass through four years of higher education preparing themselves for careers without carefully preparing for their first jobs. It happens to persons who fail to make use of networks and contacts, who fail to write persuasive résumés, who fail to investigate the job market in their chosen fields of study, who fail to prepare adequately for selection interviews, and who listen to the alluring rhetoric of campus recruiters without asking important questions. It happens to women and men of all races, colors, creeds, and religions, to persons who graduate from major and minor schools, and to persons whose senses of self-esteem and purpose unfortunately allow them to walk blindly into their own futures.

In short, it can happen to *you*.

According to a recent government study, approximately 70% of the persons working in this country are *unhappy* with their jobs.[1] Given present rates of unemployment there are approximately 10 to 15 million additional persons who are unhappy because they are not working. If these statistics are any indication of the realities they claim to represent, then we are living in a land of unrealized expectations and widespread feelings of unhappiness, not a land where "self-actualization" and "unconditional positive regard" are likely concomitants to a successful job search.

This chapter addresses the skills associated with obtaining a position in an organization. The purpose of the chapter is to debunk some common myths about the job search and selection in-

---

[1]Cited in L. Einhorn, *et al.*, *Effective Employment Interviewing: Unlocking Human Potential*. (Glenview, Ill.: Scott, Foresman, & Co., 1982), p. 26.

terviewing processes while providing a practical set of skills adaptable to any successful job search. We believe you stand a far better chance of gaining a strong foothold on a rewarding career if you approach getting your first job with these skills and understandings. If you already have a job but are among the ranks of the unhappily employed, then this chapter can show you how to improve your interviewing performances so you can locate a better job this time around.

SOME MYTHS, SOME ARCHETYPES, AND SOME TRAGIC UNTRUTHS

Since the first social science studies of interviewing were conducted in the early 1920s, there have been as many facts as fictions uncovered about who gets hired and why. For example, Mr. J.C. Penney, founder of the great department store chain, honestly believed that one, and *only* one thing was important for success during an interview—whether or not a person salted her or his food before tasting it. If the person did salt food before tasting it, it was a sure sign of snap judgments and uncritical biases Mr. Penney believed would show up on the job. If the person did not salt the food before tasting it, then the individual was one who relied on information before making decisions and was truly worthy of hire.

According to another legend concerning a financial tycoon during the 1930s, who shall go unnamed, success in an interview depended on how much attention a candidate would give the tycoon's wife over dinner. If the interviewee paid too little attention to her, she or he was unsuitable for employment because the person obviously could not tell a good thing when he or she saw it. Conversely, if the interviewee paid too much attention to her it was a sure sign of a tragic flaw—the person was too easily distracted from business by pleasure. Just how much was "enough" attention was never specified. The tycoon believed he would know it when he saw it.

These strange stories only point out two of the curious ways in which personal biases and human judgment are connected. While it may seem laughable to judge a person's professional qualifications using the salt or wife methods of analysis, both individuals who used them *believed* they worked. The literature on employment interviewing skills provides additional advisories equally suspect—from the perceived firmness of a handshake to the color of your interviewing suit, from the assertiveness with which you respond to questions to the ability to use gestures and smile while seated, the advice given is often the result of *simulated* interviewing situations in which college sophomores participate in controlled studies.[2] Other evidence strongly suggests the evaluative base for most interview settings rests with the perceived *similarity of attitudes, values, beliefs, and behaviors* between interviewer and interviewee.[3] Still other evidence argues that your choice of dress and style of nonverbal communication underscores success or failure during the interview.[4]

If we could pull together all of the advisories ever offered about success in a job interview, we would be very confused by it, and chances of finding a single individual who could perform them, even once, would be very slim. The most thorough examinations of these advisories seems to suggest that success in any interview depends *as much on the communicative style of the interviewer as it does on the performance choices made by the interviewee*.[5]

---

[2]See, for example, D. B. Goodall and H. L. Goodall, Jr., "The Employment Interview: A Selective Review of the Literature with Implications for Communication Research," *Communication Quarterly* 30, (1982), 116–23.

[3]See B. Z. Posner, "Comparing Recruiter, Student, and Faculty Perceptions of Important Applicant and Job Characteristics," *Personnel Psychology*, 34 (1981), 329–339; see also E.C. Mayfield and R.E. Carlson "Selection Interview Decisions: First Results From a Long-term Research Project," *Personnel Psychology*, 19 (1966), 41–55.

[4]See K.N. Wexley, *et. al.*, "An Applicant's Nonverbal Behavior and Student Evaluators' Judgments in a Structured Interview Setting," *Psychological Reports*, 36 (1975), 391–94; see also J. T. Molloy, *Dress for Success* (New York: Vintage, 1977).

[5]See L. Einhorn, "An Inner-View of the Job Interview: An Investigation of Successful Communicative Behaviors," *Communication Education*, 30 (1981), 217–228. Einhorn's work is based on an exhaustive treatment of the literature on employment interviewing completed in partial fulfillment for her doctorate; see her *The Rhetorical Dimensions of Employment Interviews: An Investigation of the Communicative Behaviors Contributing to Applicant Success* (Ph.D. Dissertation, Indiana University, 1979).

So what *should* you do to prepare for an interview?

Unfortunately, when persons become acquainted with the problems and paradoxes associated with doing well in an interview, they tend to elevate a romantic, potentially tragic myth to an even higher level of abstraction—the archetypal untruth. From this lofty vantage, persons as normal as you or we suddenly attribute interviewing success to Divine Guidance, Devish Demons, or The Unseen Hand of Fate. "It was meant to be this way because I've always had things pretty easy, and now it is time to pay. . . ." As any decent social scientist will tell you, when we can't adequately explain something that is very important to us, we tend to attribute it to some greater mystery.

Perhaps for this reason, and perhaps for reasons only a bit more charming, we also find persons attributing success in locating employment to "who they know." Actually, who you know can be extremely helpful during the job search process because you can learn a great deal about how this or that organization operates, and even be tipped off about an opening before it is "officially" announced. A National Public Radio broadcast during the summer of 1983 reported that *without any personal contacts at all* only about 5–7% of all job offers are based solely on résumés. Clearly it pays to know someone. The question becomes, what do you do once you know someone?

Knowing a campus recruiter or a personnel administrator or even someone high up on the corporate ladder can be of benefit by improving your chances of *getting an interview*. But it is also true that "those whom you know" will be more interested in keeping their job and reputation than in giving you one you can't do and don't deserve. Ultimately *your* performance during the interview and on the job will be the test of your real skills. If you are talented, possess the right credentials, and can perform well during the selection interview, then having friends in high places may very well give you an edge. Notice, though, it isn't "who you know" that is turning the employment key for you; he or she is only doing what any respectable recruiter or personnel officer or company person should do—providing an opportunity for a qualified candidate to prove her- or himself, and thereby aiding the organization.

One final untruth needs to be unmasked. This one begins

with the stories of Horatio Alger, which demonstrated for all time that in America good is always rewarded (J.R. Ewing wasn't born yet), especially if the good person can find some way to marry the boss's offspring. Of course we don't know what happened to the heroes of those stories when middle age set in, when the spouse's looks and the company's mismanaged fortunes were in equal and steady decline, and the old man suffered hardening of the arteries and thought snowflakes were messages from the gods. We don't have scenes of the hero spoiled by unwarranted success, terrorizing the younger men in the company and trysting with the secretaries who, like him years before, believe their corporate future depends on saying "I do" or "I will" at the right time, in the right places, with the right members of the executive family. Well, do unto others as you would have them do unto you. . . .

These days boss's daughters and sons are perhaps the least likely avenues to success. For one thing, the world has turned a few times since Horatio Alger stories were popular. Most boss's daughters and sons are career-minded individuals, and with the proper genetic pool and simple cosmetic work they don't seem inclined to fall for just anyone, regardless of how nice the anyone happens to be. Being bred into success usually inspires the need to continue living in the style to which you have become accustomed. If you do locate a marriage-minded heir or heiress, chances are that individual might be able to pass for 43 at night with light behind her or him, and not be too bright either.

If a good case can be made for *who you know* then it can be made even stronger by *what* you know. And even what you know can't help you unless you can *communicate* it effectively before, during, and after the interview. In the next section, we explore how to find out what you need to know to find gainful employment, and how to use what you know in the performances that count the most—résumé writing, answering and asking questions during the interview, and negotiating the offer.

Improving Your Interviewing I.Q.

1. What did you study (or major in) in college? Why did you select this field? Name at least five job titles related to your field of study.

2. Did you ever actively pursue career counseling in college? If so, what did you learn? If not, why not? Do you think college adequately prepares you to find your first job? Do you think colleges should be responsible for preparing you for locating employment?

3. Why do you become anxious about employment interviews? Is it because you are afraid you will get a job you don't deserve, or because you really don't want to work at all?

4. Are you afraid of interviewers? Why? Do you think they are naturally superior persons? Do you think they will see you for what you "really" are? Or are you actually afraid to face them because (a) they will ask you questions you can't answer, (b) they will question your academic and experiential preparation for a career, and (c) they will confront you with weaknesses you would prefer not to publicly acknowledge?

5. Are you willing to accept the responsibility for your career? Do you have any real idea what that means? Have you ever spent a day observing persons doing the work you claim to want to do for the rest of your life? If not, don't you think you should?

FINDING THE MARK: THE JOB SEARCH

Most persons who look for work in any field typically make three basic mistakes: (a) they fail to differentiate among organization types and behavioral styles; (b) they fail to adequately research the organization prior to submitting a résumé; and (c) they fail to subject the organization to active, noticeable, careful scrutiny. Let's examine each one of these problems in more detail.

One common assumption is that most organizations are managed in pretty much the same way. Although most persons are aware of different theories of management, finance, promotion, and organizational development, they tend to think narrowly about how organizations "in the real world" actually operate. Hence, they *fail to differentiate among organization types and behavioral styles*. In the past, many American organizations were operated in a "top-down" fashion, meaning the boss made the decisions and everyone else carried them out. Decision making was centralized in the executive ranks. Men wore suits, ties, and polished wing-tips. Women were usually relegated to the secretarial staff or the personnel office. Most people owned a briefcase, and everyone sought job security over personal gratification on the job.

Today businesses are run differently. Some organizations still cling to the older, more traditional "top-down" style of behavior, such as the military. However, in places like Huntsville, Silicon Valley, Salt Lake City, or Houston, you can find companies with multibillion dollar profits operating under vastly different systems. In some organizations, you can locate "participative management structures" including group decision making, quality circles, and project teams. Other companies are run using the "extended family structure" method, integrating all aspects of home and work life. And there are some modified "Theory Z" organizations based in part on principles of Japanese management styles that encourage corporate identity over individual identity, defer promotions while offering lifelong job security, and participative group decision making. If you are planning a career involving work in an organization, you need to investigate the varieties of management systems and behavioral styles available to you. Then ask yourself: "Is this for *me*?" Whether or not you have to wear a business suit, work within a fixed time schedule, or report to a senior official may be more important to you than you now realize.

A second faulty assumption that prevents a quality job search is that it isn't necessary or advantageous *to research the organization* prior to submitting a résumé. Hence, most persons know less about the organization they want to work for than they do about how McDonald's builds a Big Mac. Too many aspirants for the good life walk blindly into the organizations they want to work in, fill out applications, attach résumés, and then hope for the best. What if you are hired by a company with a 75% turnover rate in the entry-level ranks?

The best defense against organizational problems that can adversely affect careers is a sound strategy. *You* are the person who wants the position, so you are the person who ought to do the homework. You may want to find out what organizations do business in your area. Check out the local Chamber of Commerce, *Thomas' Register of American Manufacturers*, or *Fortune's Plant and Product Directory*. You may want to find out how the organization is financed and what fiscal shape it is in. Check out Dun and Bradstreet's *Middle Market Directory* or their *Million Dollar Directory*, *Fitch's Corporation Reports*, or *Standard & Poor's Listed Stock Reports*.

You may want to find out who works in the executive ranks, which can be found in *Standard & Poor's Register of Corporations, Directors, and Executives*.[6] You may also want to visit the companies you plan to submit résumés to, take the company tour, and collect brochures and whatever other literature you can find to familiarize you with the company. Again, your guiding question should be: "Is this for me?"

A third assumption that undermines many otherwise successful job search strategies is the assumption of *passivity*. Most persons become anxious about gaining employment (and rightfully so!), and translate their feelings of anxiety into passive actions during the investigative process. They *fail to subject the organizations under scrutiny to active, noticeable research* because they fear that "making waves" could adversely affect their opportunities. Too many would-be employees act like *victims* long before accepting the offer of employment. By "acting like victims" we mean they accept whatever the company is, has, and does to them. They are passive in their search for employment, ready to go to work for any company offering them some thin sliver of hope.

This book advocates an *active* approach to the job search. The goals of an active job search are: (a) to gain useful information about the organization, (b) to gain some idea of what working in the organization would be like and whether or not the environment is for you, and (c) to be noticed and remembered by those persons who may be in a position to help you. Rather than acting like a "go along, get along" member of the maddening, mindless crowd of employees, you need to turn your job search into a *performance* featuring you in the starring role. Following are our recommendations:

1. *Phone for a tour of the facilities with the head of the personnel division:* Explain that you are researching area organizations and would be available when it is convenient for him or her.

2. *Arrive for the tour looking like you already work there:* Here is where some of your preliminary investigations should pay off. You

---

[6]This information source can be particularly useful for women who want to see what their chances for ultimate advancement might be.

should know what style of dress is favored by the organization, and you should adapt to it. Be prompt, be courteous, and look like you know *exactly* what you are there for. The confident prospective employee naturally presents a higher profile.

3. *Begin asking questions as soon as possible after the initial greetings are exchanged:* You should prepare a list of 10 to 15 questions in advance of your tour and memorize them. An actor who must refer to a script during the performance is a hack; a professional knows her or his lines, and knows them well. Some of the questions might be:

— "What is this company's management philosophy?"
— "What is the average length of employment for someone in the _____ department?"
— "What is the average rate of turnover in the _____ department?"
— "What are three reasons for this rate of turnover?"
— "What is the company record for in-house promotions? What is the company record for promoting females (males) in these positions?"
— "How many women/men work here?"
— "Does this organization use a flex-time concept, or are employees expected to be here from 8 to 5?"
— "At what point are the retirement benefits vested? Can company stock be purchased at a discount by employees? What is the rate?"
— "How do you like working here?"
— "If you could change any one thing about this organization's routine operations, what would it be, and why would you change it?"

The answers to these questions provide you with information you need to acquire about the organization. The ability to ask the questions should also leave a lasting impression on the person conducting the tour.

If possible, request a meeting with the person who supervises the department or group you want to work with. Remember, you are not interviewing for a job, merely researching the organization. During your meeting make the following statement: "I am going to work for a company in this area. I want to be sure I choose the best organization, which is the reason for my research. I think anyone who is serious about a career in _____ should make productive use of research skills developed in college." Then ask your questions, thank the person for his or her time and cooperation, and leave promptly. Don't hang around looking homeless or you will blow the scene and ruin your chances of leaving a positive, lasting impression.

Now you are ready to make your job search official. Using the information collected, list the top five organizations in order of preference and jot down what you remember about each one of them. Whenever possible write down specific statements made by persons you talked to, and always make a note of their names. You can make productive use of these sources of information when constructing your cover letter and résumé, as well as during interviews.

The next item of your job search agenda is *money*. You need to know the going rate of pay for the job you plan to interview for in each of the five organizations you listed. To obtain this information, you need to phone the personnel departments, identify yourself, and ask for the *salary range* for the position. Do not ask what the salary *is*, ask only for the *range*. This information will become important to you if you have the opportunity to negotiate during the latter stages of the selection process. If the personnel office is reticent about providing the information, do not become offended or truculent, simply go to the library and check out the Bureau of Labor Statistic's *Annual Report*, or your professional society's data. Also collect information about benefits such as vacation time and pay, retirement, sick leave, hospitalization insurance, and investment opportunities. Once these data are collected, you are ready to begin to market yourself wisely.

YOUR BEST ADVERTISEMENT: THE CRAFT OF RÉSUMÉ WRITING

A résumé is an advertisement for yourself. Just as any other good advertisement, it should capture the attention of the target audience, appeal to its needs and expectations, and induce it to see whether or not you can satisfy its requirements. Notice we do not say a résumé is either "a sketch of your background, education, and career objectives," nor is it "a summation of the facts." It is an advertisement, designed to stimulate your audience by appealing to its needs.

There are a variety of popular guides to résumé writing. Most claim to be good because they have "proven track records," although it is difficult to know whether the persons used as evidence for the track records were successful before they used the advocated résumé style. Some guides advise a "serious" approach to the résumé, which usually translates to black ink on white paper, brief factual statements about education, work experience, and career objectives, and references. Others advocate a "contemporary" approach, which may translate to more choices of colors for paper and ink, intriguing layouts and designs, small print used for headers, livelier language, and the statement "references furnished upon request." Still other guides to the writing of résumés advocate a "combination" approach, which makes eclectic uses of serious and contemporary formats, and strives to make "a unique statement about you."

We present a somewhat different alternative (sigh). We call it "somewhat different" because although we do rely on traditional and contemporary designs, we place the emphasis on the *strategies* employed in the résumé. What we advocate is a *rhetorical* approach to résumé writing, a view of the résumé as a persuasive instrument capable of shaping the reader's impressions of you and your potentials. To use the rhetorical approach to the craft of résumé writing, you need to understand (1) the *goal* of your résumé, (2) the *audience* for it, (3) the *alternative styles* available for designing the format, and (4) some exemplary *models* of the final document. In the following sections, we provide a step-by-step method you can use to accomplish a rhetorically forceful résumé.

The Goal of the Résumé

Most persons believe a résumé should present the facts about your education, work experiences, references, and various personal details such as your address, phone number, and name. Working from this "factual" perspective, you can make your résumé read just like your obituary. You were born, lived, educated, worked, and were known by others. Because the factual perspective tends to favor the past tense, bare objective details, and chronologies, it very often makes an alive, changing person read like a recently deceased one.

The goal of the résumé is to *induce the cooperation* of the reader. You may believe the facts of your life ought to suffice or speak for themselves, but on this planet nothing that matters ought to be left to the fate of such passivity. To gain the cooperation of your reader requires careful planning and exact execution of the plan in a way that *captures* the attention of the reader(s), *pulls* him or her into the facts of your life, and then *persuades* her or him to want to interview you. You are trying to market yourself, sell yourself, advertise the product consisting of the best of what you are and what you want to become. Consider what would happen if something as precious as a diamond was marketed solely on the basis of its facts: "This is a one karat stone, acquired on 9/8/84 at a cost of $300.16 from the Alpha Mines dealer in London. We are offering it to you for only $3300.50 plus tax." Would you buy it?

To know how to induce the cooperation of your reader(s), you need to first be able to state what you want the reader to know about you as result of perusing your document. Consider these examples:

> I want the reader to know I am qualified to be an entry-level accountant.

> I want the reader to know I am the best qualified candidate for the entry-level accounting position as advertised in the Sunday paper.

> I want the reader to know I am the best qualified candidate (because I am a college graduate with a degree in accounting and experience as an auditor) for the entry-level accounting position (I work hard, do not require supervision, am organized and punctual, and understand that I will be evaluated based on my performance and social skills) as advertised in the Sunday paper (in which you listed qualifications that I possess; however, I have also visited your offices, talked with your employees, and done research concerning your organization—therefore, I represent the best informed, most qualified, and best investment you are going to find).

Which statement would you select? If you choose the third one, we agree with you. You have the proper attitude, motivation, dedication to your own career, and rhetorical spirit. Now that you have defined your goal, you need to consider the audience for your persuasive appeals.

The Audience for the Résumé

Christopher Lasch and others have argued that we are a selfish, self-centered generation of Americans.[7] In our quest for narcissistic satisfactions, we spend more time thinking about ourselves than about the audiences for ourselves. We *do* look out for Number One, probably when we should be watching out for Number Two.

Thinking about *my* career, or what *I* want to have happen is not the same thing as thinking about what *my audience* wants to have happen. As a candidate for a good job, you want to create a résumé capable of inducing the person(s) reading it to interview you. You need to consider *his or her* needs, expectations, and goals for hiring a person in the advertised position. Then you need to consider how you can meet those needs, expectations, and goals.

There are two good sources of information about your reader's requirements for a résumé. First, you can speak directly to the personnel office, to other employees, and to responsible persons in the business community and acquire direct information about the job. The second source is the job announcement itself, where, according to federal and state guidelines, the *criteria* to be used in making the employment decision must be contained. Because we have already discussed how to gain direct information from personnel officials, we will concentrate on how to read and analyze the job announcement.

A job announcement is a subtle document. Rarely will you find one that "tells the whole truth, and nothing but the truth" about the position, or the criteria used to evaluate the candidates for it. Rarely will you find an advertisement that says:

---

[7]See C. Lasch, *The Cultural of Narcissism*. (New York: W.W. Norton, 1978); see also R. Sennett, *The Fall of Public Man*. (New York: Vintage, 1978).

Are you a workaholic? Then we have the position for you! We are looking for a young, physically attractive overachiever with a B.S. degree from an Ivy League school and at least two years experience in the field. For the first six months you will work at least eighty hours a week for minimum wage without overtime pay, and then, if you meet our personal and social criteria, you might be able to work for us forever. You need to be willing to travel at a moment's notice, speak fluent Japanese, French, and Russian, be computer literate, and possess a fine wardrobe of designer originals. It is helpful if you possess a keen, analytical mind and a genuinely entertaining sense of humor. You should be familiar with all the tax laws pertaining to international trade, the fiction of Norman Mailer and Saul Bellow, and the plays of Sam Shepard. We don't approve of smoking, but do encourage social drinking after work, and no aspect of your personal life will be left unexamined. Apply immediately.

Instead, you will encounter neutral-sounding announcements that require critical scrutiny. For example, the above "honest" job announcement might actually read:

We are looking for a young, aggressive professional with a B.S. degree and a minimum of two years experience in the field to begin work immediately. The qualified candidate will be willing to work overtime and weekends, and will want to rise within our organization quickly. Knowledge of foreign languages and a neat appearance helpful.

Notice the use of highly abstract language. How "young" is young? What does "aggressive" really mean? If you have more than two years experience "in the field," are you overqualified? What if you are willing to work overtime, but prefer not to work on weekends unless you absolutely have to? How does the organization evaluate persons to see if they can "rise" in the organization? How much knowledge of foreign languages is "helpful"? What does the phrase "neat appearance" actually mean?

Decoding a job announcement is important. For example, when the term "aggressive" is used, it usually means you will have to work very hard for equally aggressive types, or that you will have to fight for your life to survive. Announcements specifying work experience in the field are misleading. Some jobs do require actual time spent in the field, but according to a recent survey of over 100 companies, the requirement can be waved in lieu of college coursework or even part-time work in a related field. If overtime/weekend duty is specified, you can be sure you will be expected to do it, often without prior warning. If you see the phrase "want to rise within the organization," you can usually decode this statement to mean "you will be conscious of favorably impressing everyone around you with your knowledge, professionalism, and social skills." And if you run across the phrase "neat appearance," it usually means only the physically attractive need apply.

Why do organizations mask their intent in abstract language? Because the federal and state governments have mandated compliance with Equal Opportunity statutes, and a variety of other laws designed to promote persons who have been discriminated against or in some way made disadvantaged. The result has been the intentional inclusion of ambiguous statements that allow any organization to discriminate equally against anyone, for virtually any reason.

So what can you do? First, read all job announcements carefully and thoroughly. Try to discern their meanings by comparing the statements in the announcement to your experiences and impressions on site. What kinds of persons work there, what statements did they make about the organization, and what sense of the place did you get from the company tour? Second, realize that whatever is written in the advertisement *will* be used to make the selection decision—it is, after all, the law. The successful résumé makes productive use of the language and skill areas specified in the announcement. If the ad says "willing to travel," so should your résumé. If it specifies a degree in accounting, and you have one, then you should clearly identify it on your résumé.[8] Once you have psyched out the job announcement, and thought carefully about your target audience, you are ready to consider alternative formats for your résumé.

[8]Never falsify anything on a résumé because it can lead to your dismissal if hired, and render your chances of ever finding employment almost impossible. If your degree is not in accounting, but you had a couple of accounting courses, stretching the truth now will only hurt you later. The best rhetorically informed résumés are also the most truthful.

Alternative Styles for Crafting the Résumé

Résumés are a modern invention. They are a product of a complex, information-based, mobile, and slightly paranoid society. These days there are so many qualified persons for all but a select few jobs that simply being able to complete the assigned task is not enough to guarantee employment. You must be able to do *more*. And the résumé is your best advertisement about how much "more" you are and can do.

A résumé is a formal statement, a brief autobiography, and a work of subtle and overt persuasion. A reader should be able to peruse your résumé in the time it takes to smoke a reduced tar cigarette, or finish a barely warm cup of decaffeinated coffee. Yet within those few, precious minutes of reading, the person holding your résumé should be moved from facts about your education, work experiences, and skills to inferences about your motivations, abilities, and personal qualities. The reader should be pleasantly induced to read your résumé, consider it, and then feel compelled to speak with you in person.

There are basically four résumé styles or formats. The *traditional format* is designed for persons who want to list the facts about themselves in black-and-white, and to create the impression of stability, reliability, and conservatism in the mind of the reader. The traditional format works best for secretarial and clerical employment opportunities, and for some managerial, accounting, and professorial positions with high-status firms or conservative colleges and universities (see Figure 2.1).

The *modified traditional format* is designed for persons who want to create conservative, stable impressions about themselves, but who have accomplished goals (i.e., high grades in school, leadership positions, rapid advancement, etc.) worthy of mention on the résumé. The modified traditional format is particularly useful for aspiring managers, marketeers, and advertising, public relations, and graphics specialists who want to obtain work with a more prestigious company than the one they are currently employed by (see Figure 2.2).

The *contemporary format* is designed for persons who want to present a résumé capable of displaying their creative and individualistic talents. The contemporary format seems to work best for individuals possessing backgrounds in the liberal arts/ humanities, with limited work experiences, or for women who have recently acquired a college degree after spending part of their lives as secretaries, clerks, homemakers, or teachers (see Figure 2.3). However, it can also be used by persons with backgrounds in business who want to draw attention to their unique qualifications (see Figure 2.4).

The *artistic format* is designed for persons who desire careers in the fine and performing arts (i.e., music, drama, broadcasting, film, creative writing, and art). These résumés tend to be unusual in their choices of paper color and ink, and in their use of graphics (see Figure 2.5).

One final word about résumés. Because résumés should be designed for *a specific job*, we do not recommend the use of *one*, and only one, format. Our experience strongly suggests you have a far better chance of getting an interview if you individually tailor the résumé to fit the job you are applying for. Having one résumé you submit to 50 different organizations is seldom a good practice. We believe you ought to carefully design a résumé for each job, adapting the choice of format and the language used to describe your background to the needs and expectations of the particular organization. In the next section, we explain what you should do between submitting your résumé and participating in an interview.

HANDLING SELECTION INTERVIEWS: TWENTY QUESTIONS AND HOW TO ANSWER THEM

You've done your homework. You are familiar with the job market, you have targeted the specific organizations with which you plan to interview. You have crafted résumés worthy of respect. You have mailed the résumés and cover letters, and now you wait for responses to your strategy.

Waiting is the harshest penalty of employment interviewing. Even if you are turned down for a job you are left with a sense of completion to complement your rage or frustration. But just *waiting* has no complementary emotions. You simply wait. Should you call the personnel office to ask if they have received your application? Should you apply for other positions you really aren't interested

Figure 2.1 The Traditional Format

                        HAROLD O. MELVIN

                        610 S. Front St.
                        Harrisburg, PA 17017
                        (717)-555-5555

Born: January 1, 1960   SS#: 211-44-4555
Harrisburg, PA   Health: Excellent

                        EDUCATION

    Presently completing M.S. degree in Finance at
    Bucknell University (degree expected 6/86).

    Bachelor of Science in Business Administration
    from Shippensburg State College, May 1982.

                    WORK EXPERIENCE

    May 1982 - Present   First United National Bank
    Loan officer   Harrisburg, PA 17017
                            Duties include interviewing
                            clients, helping clients
                            complete applications, dis-
                            persing funds, handling bad
                            debts.

    June 1978 - May 1982   The Old Towne Bank & Trust Co.
    Bank teller/cashier   Shippensburg, PA 17200
                            Part-time work while attending
                            college. Duties included handling
                            and counting monies, making trans-
                            actions, and general banking pro-
                            cedures. Resigned to accept pre-
                            sent position.

    June 1977 - May 1978   Hamburger Heaven, Inc.
    Counter Clerk   Harrisburg, PA 17017
                            Part-time work while completing
                            high school education. Duties
                            included handling and processing
                            customer orders, dealing with
                            complaints, handling money, and
                            general clean-up assignments.
                            Resigned to attend college.

                        REFERENCES

Professor H.B. Ticket   Mrs. Alma Johnson   Mr. John Smith
110 Old Hall   First United Bank   Old Towne Bank & Trust
Bucknell University   100 River Street   10 Main Street
Lewisburg, PA 17551   Harrisburg, PA 17017   Shippensburg, PA 17257

Figure 2.2 Modified Traditional Format

HELEN H. HUMPHREYS

Home Address	*Business Address*
1000 Greenlawn Pkwy. #121	*2525 New Business Center, N.E.*
Dubuque, IA 52001	*Dubuque, IA 52001*
(319)-555-2211	*(319)-555-8899*
DOB: 10/17/57	*SS#: 567-44-5767*
Single	*Health: Excellent*

Career Objective: To obtain a responsible managerial position with a multi-national firm specializing in fashion merchandising.

Education: B.S.B.A. degree in Marketing (cum laude) from The University of Iowa in June 1985. College of Business Administration honors (1985); WHO'S WHO AMONG STUDENTS IN AMERICAN UNIVERSITIES AND COLLEGES (1985); Wilson Scholarship recipient (1983 - 85); Dean's List all terms.

    Special competencies: Consumer behavior, promotional strategies, advertising media, small group communication, fluent in German, French, and Japanese.

Work Experience:

June 1985 - Present	*Asst. Manager, FUTURISTIC FASHIONS, INC. Dubuque, Iowa 52001. In charge of evening and weekend operations, supervise three sales personnel, keep all financial records.*
May 1979 - January 1983	*Sales Clerk, Sears & Roebuck Company, Ames, Iowa 52676. Full-time work while attending college part-time. Resigned when awarded honors scholarship to complete formal education.*
July 1975 - May 1979	*Secretary, Jones & Johnson, Inc., Dubuque, Iowa 52001. Full-time work for large legal firm. Duties included typing, filing, delivering documents, entertaining clients. Resigned to gain experience in sales field and attend college.*

Hobbies: Tennis, swimming, reading, practicing language skills.

Personal Data: Height: 5'7"   Weight: 125

REFERENCES AVAILABLE UPON REQUEST.

Figure 2.3 Contemporary Résumé I

Résumé of

DONNA LAUREN BENJAMIN

<u>*Home Address:*</u>   <u>*Business Address:*</u>

1010 Humes Avenue, N.E.   *Computer Sciences Corp.*
Huntsville, AL 35801   *Huntsville, AL 35805*
(205)-555-6645   *(205)-555-1000 x 385*

Date of Birth: 22 April 1953   *Health: Excellent*
Marital Status: Married (no children)   *SS#: 193-30-5087*

PROFESSIONAL EXPERIENCE

March 1982 - Present   *Computer Sciences Corporation*
                                                              Executive Plaza
                                                              Huntsville, AL 35805
                                                              <u>*Job Title: Technical Editor*</u>

*<u>Primary responsibilities</u> include assessing technical and
human resources necessary for producing quality technical
documents and coordinating the work of technical writers,
proofreaders, graphics personnel, word processing operators, and QA representatives. Responsible for editing
MMICS (Maintenance Management Inventory Control Systems)
for military conversion to UNIVAC systems.*

*<u>Accomplishments</u> include completion of all documents on
or before scheduled deadlines, promotion to task leader
on two major CSC projects (MMICS and Training Manuals)
and successful resolution of group conflicts caused by
interpersonal and task-related problems.*

August 1980 - March 1982   *The University of Alabama in Huntsville*
                                                              School of Administrative Science and
                                                              School of Primary Medical Care
                                                              Huntsville, AL 35899
                                                              <u>*Job Title: Writer/Researcher/Interviewer*</u>

*<u>Primary responsibilities</u> included research and writing
of technical documents and articles concerning a funded
study of nutritional and medical problems faced by elderly
citizens of Northern Alabama; conducted screening interviews and analyses of statistical data relevant to the
project. Resigned when grant was completed.*

*<u>Accomplishments</u> included completion of the funded work
on schedule and co-authorship of two research articles
based on the study. During this time I also completed
my graduate coursework at UAH.*

Figure 2.3 (Cont)

Donna Lauren Benjamin
Résumé 2

OTHER WORK EXPERIENCE:

June 1973 - August 1977   *Capital Blue Cross*
                                             100 Pine Street
                                             Harrisburg, PA 17017
                                             Job Title: Contract Specialist

   Responsibilities included writing and editing health
   maintenance contracts and preparing technical docu-
   ments for the Staff Counsel and Vice-President of
   the company.

   Accomplishments included four years of outstanding
   appraisal reviews and several merit raises based
   on job performance. Resigned to attend college
   full-time.

EDUCATION

August 1980 - August 1982   *The University of Alabama in Huntsville*
                                             School of Administrative Science
                                             Huntsville, AL 35899
                                             Degree Granted: M.A.S. (August 1982)

   Successfully completed course of study leading to
   the Master of Administrative Science degree with
   emphases in management of human resources and
   computer science. Final GPA: 2.75 (3.0 scale).

August 1977 - May 1980   *The Pennsylvania State University*
                                             College of Human Development
                                             University Park, PA 16802
                                             Degree Granted: B.S. (May 1980)

   Graduated cum laude with final GPA of 3.22 (4.0 scale)
   in Nutrition Science; completed additional coursework
   in communication arts, including small group problem-
   solving, interpersonal communication, and composition.

SKILLS

   *Technical writing and editing (familiar with a variety of professional
   style manuals and constraints, including NASA, the United States
   Air Force Technical Manuals, the United States Army Corps of En-
   gineers Technical Manuals, APA, MLA).

   *Communicating for results (professional interviewing, directing the
   work of others, giving technical instructions, problem-solving
   group interaction).

References and article reprints available upon request.

Figure 2.4 Contemporary Résumé II

GREG SUMMERS

16 Bluewood Drive Evanston, Ill. 60202 (312)-555-3232

career objective

Staff accountant with reputable firm where the ability to complete assignments using creative computer programming and the skill of dealing effectively with stressful situations and persons is needed and rewarded.

successful accounting experience

Presently employed as an Accounting Assistant for Watson, Wilson, and Pike (20 hours/week since June 1984). Handle programming assignments for public accounts, and perform intricate auditing work. Have been offered permanent position, but prefer to seek a career with a larger, expanding firm.

accounting education

Will receive my B.S. in Accounting from Northwestern University in June 1985. Have completed a minor in computer science with extensive independent study work in innovative software design for accounting and financial data. Maintained a 3.5 (4.0 scale) GPA overall with 3.92 in major and 4.0 in minor. President, Tau Alpha fraternity 1984-85; member, Young Republican Club 1983-85. Elected to Accounting and Computer Science Honoraries. Will take the CPA exam in August 1985.

interesting facts

Developed mail-order computer software game and financial records company in June 1983. Company now distributes over 50 programming packages to over 270 clients in the United States and Canada. Have travelled extensively in the Americas and in Asia, and am fluent in Spanish, Japanese, and several dialects of Chinese. Run 5 miles a day, work out with Nautilus equipment three times a week, and enjoy participating in wrestling, gymnastics, and soccer.

references

Available upon request.

Figure 2.5 Artistic Résumé

jay emmett johnstone

professional actor

Agent: Gloria Stern 1230 Park Avenue New York, NY 10028

professional experience

<u>*Romeo*</u> *in New Atlantis production of "Romeo & Juliet," 1984-85;*
<u>*Oedipus*</u> *in Louisville Theatre League production of "Oedipus
the King," 1983-84;* <u>*Kev*</u> *in UNC-Greensboro production of "Gimme
Shelter," summer 1983;* <u>*Charley Brown*</u> *in UNC-Greensboro production of "You're a Good Man, Charley Brown," spring, 1982;
various <u>mime</u> roles in Appalachian Touring Company summer
productions, 1982; various supporting roles in undergraduate
productions at The University of Texas-Austin, 1979-81.*

professional education

*MFA in Theatre, The University of North Carolina-Greensboro,
1983; production thesis of Tennessee Williams' "Summer in Smoke;"
final GPA 3.5 (4.0 scale).*

*BFA in Theatre Arts, The University of Texas-Austin, 1982;
major in Acting; minor in Theatre History; final GPA: 3.3
(4.0 scale). President, Alpha Psi Omega, 1981-82.*

Height: 6'   *Hair: Blonde*
Weight: 170   *Eyes: Blue*

```
-----------------------
|                     |
|                     |
|      PHOTO          |
|                     |
|      HERE           |
|                     |
|                     |
|                     |
-----------------------
```

*specialties: serious dramatic roles, light comedy, mime, tapdancing,
.swordfighting, foreign accents (Cockney, French, aristo-
cratic German), gymnastics.*

Member, Actors' Equity

in, just to fill in the time? Should you take a short vacation to clear your head? Should you clean your apartment?

The answer to all the above questions is *no*. However, there is something you can and should do between applying for the job and being interviewed. It is something so simple and yet so necessary that it can go unnoticed. This simple something is to *prepare for the interview*. Without completing this step of the process, even a handsome résumé and good market research can backfire.

Most persons we talk to claim they do prepare for interviews. However, upon closer questioning we often find their preparation consists of *thinking* about the job, *worrying* about the interview, and *hoping* for the best. This does not constitute interview preparation. Preparation consists of a systematic plan for developing cogent answers to stock issues and questions, and a general strategy for dealing with more difficult, spontaneous queries. Preparation is an active rehearsal for your interviewing performance.

In this section, we consider preparing for, and performing in the selection interview process. First, we will discuss the *structure* of the routine employment interview. Second, we will show you how to deal with 20 stock issues that can spell success or failure for your career.

Understanding the Structure of the Interview

Basically there are two kinds of interviews—the structured and the unstructured. The structured interview is the favored method for the seasoned interviewing professional because it is more reliable, more justifiable, and takes less time overall than the unstructured variety.[9] The structured approach consists of well-researched questions whose phrasing is carefully chosen to gain the most important information from the respondent. The structured interview is precise (all or most of the questions are prepared in advance), equitable (all the interviewees were asked the same basic ques-

---

[9]See B.M. Cohen and J.M. Etheridge, "Recruiting's Main Ingredient," *Journal of College Placement* (1975), 75–77; see also T. Moffat, *Selection Interviewing for Managers* (New York: Harper & Row, 1979), Chapter 3.

tions), and reliable (different interviewers tend to obtain the same results).[10]

The unstructured interview is dangerous and unreliable. By "unstructured" we mean the interviewer has no clear plan for asking questions, evaluating answers, or making selection decisions. The unstructured interview is characterized by (a) spontaneity in the method of questioning, (b) emphasis on the physical appearance and overt personality of the interviewees, (c) ad-hoc discussions of news, weather, and sports interjected into the interview, and (d) prejudice against interviewees who do *not* closely resemble the attitudes, values, beliefs, and behaviors of the interviewer.

Why do unstructured interviews still exist if they are unreliable and prejudiced? One researcher, Cal Downs, points out that many interviewers actually believe they can and should make insightful interviewing decisions simply by talking to the interviewee.[11] Unfortunately, research clearly demonstrates that what these "interviewing professionals" are really doing is looking for carbon copies of themselves.[12]

We believe you have the best opportunity to make a favorable impression in a structured interview. This doesn't mean structured interviews are easy; it means their structure allows you the best opportunities to field questions well. If you are prepared for the stock issues, and understand the basic structure of the structured interview approach, you can rehearse a strong, productive performance.

The structure of the structured interview is *deductive*, usually beginning with broad open-ended questions such as "Tell me about yourself," and moving systematically toward specific questions designed to probe into important areas concerning your background, education, work experiences, training, professional goals, and general personality (see Figure 2.6).

[10]See E.C. Mayfield, S.H. Brown, and B.W. Hamstra, "Selection Interviewing in the Life Insurance Industry: An Update of Research and Practice," *Personnel Psychology*, 33 (1980), 725–739.

[11] C.W. Downs, "Perceptions of the Selection Interview," *Personnel Administration*, (May-June 1969), 8–23.

[12]See D.B. Goodall and H.L. Goodall, Jr., "The Employment Interview," *Communication Quarterly*, 30 (1982), 116–123.

Figure 2.6

Entrance, handshake, being seated . . .

Explanation of the company, the job description, and the method for conducting the interview . . .

General Background Questions

1. Tell me about yourself.
2. And so then you went to college.
   a. What do you believe you learned about ——————— as a result of studying ——————— at ———————?
   b. What else did you accomplish while going to school?
3. How did your experiences working at ——————— during school contribute to your practical understanding of this job?
   a. What skills/competencies did you acquire while working at ——————— doing ———————?
   b. Is there anything else I should know about your work experiences?
4. Internal review of questions/answers.

Specific Questions Based on Earlier Information

5. Why do you think you can do this job for us?
6. If you could do any job in any organization, what would it be?
7. What are your professional/personal goals?

Hypothetical Questions

8. Here is a situation you may encounter on this job. What do you think you would do?
9. Why did you select that response?
10. What three influences might have altered your answer?

Review and Internal Summary

11. I think I have gained some useful information thus far. Let me see if I can summarize what you've told me.
12. Do you have any questions?

End of the Interview

13. Explanation of when decisions will be made and how the candidate will be informed.

Exit

BEGINNING — MIDDLE — ENDING

As you can see from Figure 2.6, the structured interview follows a chronological, biographical pattern. The general background questions allow the interviewer to hear your life's story in abbreviated form. From the answers you give to where you were reared, educated, and trained, the interviewer can develop a plan for getting to specific questions relevant to the job you are interviewing for. Hence, the answers you provide to these initial queries are very important because they set the stage for all other questions during the interview. You can afford to leave nothing to chance. Through careful preparation for these basic issues in the beginning of the interview, you can actively shape the interviewer's perceptions of you, your background, and your potentials. Now let's examine the 20 questions that you need to prepare for prior to the selection interview.

Twenty Questions

1. *Tell me about yourself.* This is probably the most dangerous question you can be asked during any job interview. Your answer will spell out your background, what interests you, and some of the reasons why you are what you claim to be. Mistakes are most often made when you disclose *too much* about your personal history, including feelings about family and friends, past work experiences, and ideals. Too much information given without regard for purpose of the interview (to gain employment, not to gain a friend), or the goals of the interviewer (to gain appropriate data upon which to base a selection decision, not to counsel you about your problems or help you find a job) is seldom productive.

Most authorities agree the best way to prepare an answer for this question, or others of its ilk, is to stick pretty close to the details on your résumé. Find a theme that can unite where you were born, reared, and your early education, and show how each detail of your life contributed to your present plans for employment. For example, if you travelled a great deal during your upbringing and learned how to adapt to new places and people, beginning your response with the statement "I have always been a person who could adapt to new situations . . ." can be productive. This approach is especially useful when dealing with an interviewer who may not have taken the time to carefully read over your résumé— you gain an edge by providing a productive perspective on the data revealed. Limit your response to 20–40 seconds.

2. *How did your family influence your choice of a career (or a college)?* Be careful, everything you say in response to this one will be interpreted psychologically, even if the interviewer's only knowledge of the subject came in an intro course 20 years ago. This question is designed to weed out "Momma's boys" and "Daddy's girls" from consideration. It is also designed to see how independent you may be. One good way to answer this question is to point out how you were equally influenced by both parents, but chose your own career: "Of course I have always listened to the advice given to me by my parents. My mother wanted me to become a surgeon, my father preferred law. As you can see, I am neither a doctor nor a lawyer, but I also have no regrets. I think it an accomplishment that I managed to forge my own life without damaging the feelings of either parent, don't you?"

3. *Why did you attend college at* —————? Good question! Many persons do *not* make active decisions about their schooling—they are most influenced by convenient locations, or because their boyfriend/girlfriend goes there. Whatever the reason was, during the interview it is important to demonstrate your reasoning ability: "I chose Shepherd College because it is a small liberal arts school that places emphasis on quality teaching. I turned down an honors scholarship to the University of Maryland because it is a large, unfriendly campus with a strict research orientation. Research is fine for graduate students, but undergraduates usually get stuck with teaching assistants and I wanted quality in the classrooms I attended."

4. *How did you decide to major in* —————? Here is a question that requires a good bit of thought. It is not a good idea to simply mimic the spirit of the times (e.g., "I selected accounting because I knew I could always get a job . . ."; or "I chose engineering because the average starting salary is about $30,000.") Nor is it a good idea to have done what others told you to do (e.g., "My parents wanted me to become a business tycoon"). Again, reveal *good rea-*

sons for your decision: "I majored in English because I felt it would provide me with a sound basis in critical thinking, decision making, and writing skills necessary to any productive career. I minored in finance because I needed to gain an understanding of how monetary systems operate, and to ground my education in the humanities with some practical knowledge."

5. *If you could do it all over again, what major (or college) would you choose?* Watch out! This question is as loaded as Falstaff.. Your answer should reaffirm your original decision, but perhaps with minor refinements brought about by your maturity. "I would select business administration again. However, I would enroll in more computer programming and organizational communication courses." Do not say you would completely change your career tracks because if that is the case you should have done so long before graduation.

6. *Do you believe your grade point average accurately reflects your abilities?* This is an easy question to answer if you were an "A" student, more difficult if you were a "B−" one. The borderline student must provide some justification for his or her marks, despite the obvious fact that they were passing marks. "I don't think so. I went to college adequately prepared, but I fooled around too much during my freshman and sophomore years. It wasn't until I took a course in ————— that my career possibilities opened up and I became serious about my education. Since that time I made significantly better grades, which I believe is indicative of my learning potential." Never blame poor grades on poor instructors, or on personal problems. You will sound too much like a complainer, even if you are being honest.

7. *What are your future educational goals?* This is a question that requires prior research of the organization. Find out whether or not the company sponsors continuing education courses, or endorses employees' entry into graduate degree programs. If they don't, then you should say something like this: "I have no plans at the present time, although someday I may pursue an MBA to enhance my knowledge of current trends in the field." And "someday" should be at least 8 to 10 years away. If the organization does encourage continuing education, you might say: "I believe a valuable employee is always a student in his or her field. I would like

very much to pursue my mastery of ——————— as soon as possible. I know this organization offers incentives for obtaining work-related education, which is one reason I feel at home here."

8. *Name three things you learned in school that will be of practical value to you on this job.* Feel suddenly uncomfortable? This question will make the brightest person tense because it is hard to know what the person asking the question needs to hear. Our experience indicates a preference for (a) processes or techniques you've mastered, and/or (b) practical skills you can perform. For example: "I believe my greatest source of knowledge springs from an ability to make rational decisions. I am familiar with a variety of problem-solving and decision-making techniques, such as PERT/CPM, Standard Agenda, and decision-treeing. Second, I think I have demonstrated my ability to resolve work-related conflicts by im-plementing a goal-oriented method for reducing the inherent semantic ambiguities that undergird any conflict situation. And third, I guess I would have to say my thorough understanding of software analysis procedures, including my ability to write in FORTRAN and COBOL." This question should *not* be answered by referencing individual courses (the interviewer will seldom be familiar with them), specific instructors (you will sound like a groupie), or broad subjects (saying you know a lot about "con-sumer behavior" opens a line of tough questions you may want to avoid).

9. *What do you think your work experiences have contributed to your ability to perform any job?* All work experiences are valuable because they should teach you the value of being punctual, reliable, adap-tive, and strategic. Do not discount time spent flipping burgers at Wendy's or pumping gas for Exxon. If *you* treat your past work experiences as something you'd rather forget, then your negative attitude will negatively influence the interviewer (who may also have flipped his or her share of burgers).

Women too often make the mistake of discounting their se-cretarial years as if all they learned how to do was sit properly and type. The meaning of work experiences is interpreted by the indi-viduals involved; if you have interpreted your work history nega-tively, there is no reason to suppose the interviewer won't be in-clined to agree with you. However, if you can provide a fresh perspective on what you did, and why you did it, then you win bonus points for being insightful: "In high school I learned how to type, so when I wanted to supplement my income during college I became a typing specialist for Kelly Services. I learned how to adapt to unique circumstances, meet deadlines, and also acquired some ability to run word processing machines. I also had the opportunity to work for a wide variety of organizations— manufacturing, high-tech, government agencies, defense contractors, and so forth. I think my early work experiences have given me a fuller appreciation of the available options in my career field, and that is why I am here talking to you."

10. *Why do you want to leave your present position (or why did you leave your last job)?* Technically this is not a kosher question. However it does need to be productively answered if it is asked. Avoid disclosing personal reasons such as "I can't get promoted." Also avoid spreading rumors or gossip about your present or past employers, or the company in general. Anything negative you cite will count against you no matter how true it may be. Focus on your career: "I am interested in gaining experience with your firm because I can acquire new skills in ————." If you were laid off, say so. If you were fired, try to act like you learned from the experience: "I lost my last job because I made the mistake of not taking the chain of command seriously enough. I got impatient and tried to expedite matters in my own way when I shouldn't have done so. I have learned the importance of respecting organizational hierarchies now, and I don't anticipate any difficulties working here."

11. *If you could do anything you wanted to do, for any organization you can think of, what would it be?* This question presents a logical problem. If you are honest you may reveal too much about your personal goals and lose the job. If you say only that "this is the job I have always wanted," and it is an entry-level position, you come off like an underachiever. It is best to focus your answer on work in your chosen field (or the field you are trying now to enter), and give a future-oriented answer: "I would someday like to rise to executive ranks of this organization in the area of marketing research. However, right now I can't think of a better way to reach

my goal than to begin with this position and work very hard at it." Avoid admitting that (a) you'd like to retire young and open your own business, (b) you'd really like to be writing best-selling fiction, or (c) you want to run for elected office.

12. *Tell me what your basic responsibilities were while working for* ——. This request can cause problems because "the grass is always greener. . . ." and what you *were* doing will probably seem less important, less exciting, less professional than what you are interviewing for. So you tend to devalue it. Unfortunately, this perceptual flaw may lead the interviewer to also think less of what you have done. If you say "Oh, I just worked there doing technical writing and answering questions about where commas go," then your view of the job is likely to negatively influence the interviewer. If you say "I am currently a technical writer, and my duties include organizing all technical documents for a $210 million dollar government contract, editing work for computer efficiency, and resolving disputes brought on by misinterpretations of stylistic details," then you sound a mite better.

13. *Why do you want to work here?* Here is the question you should be waiting for. If you have done your homework, you should have enough original and comparative data about this organization to impress the interviewer. So your answer could be: "Well, I want to work here because this position seems especially suited to my background and interests. Furthermore, I have researched the top five organizations in this area and yours clearly excells in ————, ————, and ————. With my professional skills and leadership potential, and your record of success in ————, we should be a perfect match." Avoid saying "I need a job and this is one," or something equally mundane. Also avoid over-complimenting the company, particularly if you aren't sure how good they really are. Telling Number 2 they are Number 1 only shows your lack of research and doesn't favorably recommend you.

14. *Why should I hire you?* Don't be fooled by this question. It is not as obvious as it seems, primarily because it is usually asked *prior to* a "test" question (see next entry). What the interviewer is doing is allowing you enough rope to hang yourself, or to prove

yourself—you choose. If you say wild, wonderful things about yourself that cannot be easily documented or demonstrated, then in a few minutes time you will probably look like a fool. If you claim skills and competencies you don't have, you will look even worse. Answer the question honestly, and directly: "You should hire me because I have the education and work background to do the job well, and I am willing to go to work on Monday. You could hire someone else with similar qualifications, but then I could also go to work for somebody else, and that wouldn't make either of us happy, or in the long run satisfied. I can do the job and I want very much to do it."

15. *The test or hypothetical question.* These questions come in an infinite variety of forms and styles. One common example is the "what would you do if . . ." format, and another is the "I have a problem, a real problem, and I wonder how you might approach it if you were me." You are being asked to demonstrate your competencies. Our experience clearly shows that *the reasoning processes used to think through the question are far more important than the answer you actually give.* Explain what you would take into consideration, what the goal of the plan would be, and what contingencies you might have to deal with if your original plan didn't work out. Avoid saying you need "more time," or that you would "ask the boss for guidance," as these choices only show you as a reticent decision maker.

16. *The either/or question.* This question also comes in a variety of styles, but the format is always the same because it includes or implies a forced choice between two opposites: "Would you prefer to make a lot of money or to serve your country?" The best answer to any of these either/or questions is usually both/and: "I think it is possible, and laudible, to do both. Making money is important to stimulate the economy, and stimulating the economy is important to the economic health of the nation."

17. *Define success (or challenging work, or job satisfaction, etc.).* Questions of definition are designed to find out what motivates you at work. You should prepare answers that reflect a broad range of options, such as "Success means accomplishing the job to the best of my ability and to my supervisor's satisfaction. It also means

valuing the work I do, and providing a source of self-esteem that will ultimately carry over into my personal life." This format for a response should immediately be followed by an example drawn from your work or collegiate experiences.

18. *Tell me what makes a good —— (manager, engineer, teacher, scientist, artist, etc.).* This question is usually followed by "Now tell me what makes a *great* one." For this reason you need to avoid abstractions such as "enjoying my work," or "getting along well with others." Put the emphasis on performance of assigned duties, and excellence in achieving results.

19. *What are your greatest professional strengths?* This question is often followed by "Now tell me about your weaknesses." Again, be modest in your tally of strengths, and demonstrate self-awareness in your tally of weaknesses without relying overmuch on destructive self-disclosures. "My strengths include having the background and desire to succeed by accomplishing assigned duties and tasks, regardless of what it takes to get the job done. My major weakness is probably the inclination to give others a second chance or maybe to overwork myself."

20. *Do you have any questions?* You should indeed have questions, but they should *not* focus initially on salary or benefits. Instead you should be interested in the organization's opportunities for advancement in their field, the interviewer's perceptions of the company, and anything else your research efforts might have uncovered which require clarification. Wait until the end of the interview to bring up the question of salary and benefits, and then understand that initial interviewers almost never determine salaries.

These 20 questions provide a basic guide to a structured interview format. To prepare for these questions you should follow these guidelines: (a) answer the questions succinctly, (b) provide an example drawn from your education or work experiences that demonstrates the truth of your answer, and then (c) when possible, ask for feedback from the interviewer (e.g., "Have I fully answered that question?")

Rehearse these answers. You should be able to adapt the

basic strategies you develop to different interviewers and interviewing situations once you become comfortable with the script. Here are some final advisories about performing in the job interview:

- Maintain eye contact with the interviewer without trying to stare him or her down.
- Dress for the interview as if you already are working for the organization, in the job category you are interviewing for.
- Try to maintain a relaxed appearance, and when possible smile and make use of gestures (avoid looking "frozen in your seat").
- Lean slightly forward and orient your body facing the interviewer.
- Always be courteous, polite, and follow the rules for appropriate public behavior, including using "yes sir/m'am", avoiding discussions of politics and religion, and avoiding untoward words, street language, or jargon.
- Make sure to ask when the decision will be made and how you will be notified.
- Try to end the interview with the statement "I really do want this job." It is easier to hire an enthusiastic person.
- Leave promptly after the end of the interview, and be sure to thank the interviewer for his or her time and cooperation.

AFTER THE INTERVIEW

The door closes. You pause, smile politely at the receptionist, and walk the short steps to the main elevator. You are oblivious to the look and sound of others as you leave the building confident that it was a good interview. Your chances of getting this job couldn't be better.

On the way home, though, you are consumed with post-interview blues. Your skin feels slick with perspiration and the hairs on the back of your neck are still at attention. Your mind whizzes and careens off of specific images remembered from the interview while wrestling with another part of your mind that advises "forget it, try to relax, relax. . . ."

Although the interview is over, the experience is not yet complete. The ordeal of waiting for the final decision lays ahead.

The interviewer said it would be two weeks, that she would call. What should you do in the meantime?

Again the possibilities seem only too clear. Clean the apartment, visit relatives, read a book, vegetate with the tube, walk a lot. Or you could *review your performance in the interview*.

Maybe you won't get the job. You do have other job opportunities, and you do have other résumés being perused. A good actor always takes notes on his or her performances. In the privacy of your living room, it is possible to obtain a degree of objectivity about the merits and flaws in your interviewing performance. Completing this kind of analysis can improve your understanding of the interview situation, and prepare you for better performances next time.

1. Review the structure for the interview. Write down everything you can remember from the time you walked in until you left in the order in which they occurred.

2. Underscore the questions that were difficult to answer. Try to recall exactly what you said and did while answering it. Did you maintain eye contact? Did you include a series of "um, ah, well, I uhs" in your response? Were you able to document your answer with an example drawn from work or educational experiences? Did you remain calm?

3. Re-examine the questions you felt you answered excellently. What were the salient characteristics of the questions—did they pertain to your career objectives, educational background, work experiences, or skills? Why do you feel you answered them well? Did you feel more comfortable than you did with other questions? Were you able to document your case with more vivid examples?

4. Write down any other problems you experienced. Were there empty moments during which time you didn't know what to say or do? What prompted them? Where did your rehearsal pay off, and where was it deficient? What new or unusual questions were you asked?

5. Make a list of improvements for your interviewing behavior. Now, while you are waiting for the call, why not spend some time

rehearsing those improvements? You will also be more attractive to any prospective employer if you have another offer, or at least one pending.

Take the initiative!
Don't act like a victim of the interview!
Proceed with your career!!

Tough Questions for Seasoned Interviewees

1. Is it possible to answer the questions "Tell me about yourself" without imposing a retrospective order on the events and experiences you isolate? Does this mean you are being strategic, regardless of the order you impose? Does it indicate you ought to choose the best possible organizing format, and then find the events to complete it? Or should you add up the events you want to talk about and then see what your life amounts to? Which approach is more truthful?

2. If you know physical attractiveness is important in any interview and you can use your physical assets to strategic advantage, would you do so? If you do use your attractiveness to gain employment, do you think if you suddenly become less attractive your employer has the right to terminate your employment? Why not?

3. Are we ever hired solely on the basis of our professional skills? Do you really believe you should be? Does this mean you are demanding a higher (or lower) standard of ethical behavior from the company interviewing you, and the interviewer, then you generally expect from yourself? Does this make you feel uneasy?

4. When you exchange conversation with a stranger, are you actually "interviewing" her or him? Do you use your impressions gained from that conversation to form a general opinion of the person's character or worth? Is it because you act this way that you are never completely at ease while being interviewed yourself, or, for that matter, when talking to strangers?

5. When is an interview actually over? Does it ever end? If so, how do you know the ending when it happens? Is it because you are suddenly accepted socially or because you have demonstrated your professional skills? Are you certain? Think again.

chapter three
THE ABSOLUTELY ESSENTIAL SKILLS

" 'Would you tell me, please, which way I ought to go from here?' [asked Alice] 'That depends a good deal on where you want to go,' said the Cat."

—LEWIS CARROLL

"The first condition of having to deal with somebody at all is to know with whom one has to deal."

—GEORG SIMMEL

"Who would succeed in the world should be wise in the use of pronouns. Utter the You twenty times, where you once utter the I.

—JOHN HAY

THE CULTURE OF ORGANIZATIONAL REALITY

An organizational culture is a set of beliefs, values, attitudes, and acceptable behaviors that must be learned if you are to succeed in any organization. These are the essential skills of making it because they lie at the interface of task and social skills, the loose integration of *who* you are with *what* you are in the eyes of others who share your professional space and time.

53

To learn the culture of any organization you enter is not simple, it is subtle. You won't find it on an organizational chart or in a strategic planning report, but instead in the stories, metaphors, rituals, rites, and ceremonies that define the particular *language usage, symbol systems, and communicative patterns* of the persons working there. To make it in any organization you have to become a user of the common language, a knower of the symbolic properties of words and numbers that have special meanings to the users, and above all, you must become an adept *performer* of those cultural understandings.

This chapter is about learning the absolutely essential skills of making it in any organization. It is designed to help you develop what David Reisman called "internal radar," the invisible antennae needed to tune you in to the culture you enter, as an immigrant from a distant shore, every time you enter an American organization.[1] This chapter is designed to help you develop your professional competencies where they count—at the level of understanding the people you work with and for. First, we examine the absolutely essential skill of story and joketelling, including knowing when to laugh. Second, we investigate how to identify the wise among the common and learn the prevailing cultural wisdom and ways of behaving necessary to organizational survival. Third, we provide our guide to organizing yourself, your work space, and your time. And finally, we deal with a variety of special understandings, from handling emergencies to taking orders from superiors.

JOKES, STORIES, AND THEIR CULTURAL SIGNIFICANCE

On Joking and Laughter

One of the basic rules of organizational life is that most of the day spent at work is ordinary, mundane, dull, routine, and mildly

---

[1]See D. Reisman, N. Glazer, and R. Denney, *The Lonely Crowd* (New York: Doubleday & Company, 1950).

painful. Most of us do live lives of quiet desperation in the organizations that employ us, the families that nurture and torture us, all the days of our lives. Work after all, is work. Sometimes you hate the thought of getting out of bed to face the horror of the day, and sometimes your bad days seem to last forever. Sometimes you lose when it is important to win, and sometimes winning seems to be beyond our control. But bad days can be endured and losing can sometimes be turned into victory if you know how and when to laugh. In every organizational culture, humor was a special place, an almost sacred place, because a good joke or story can break the dullness of the absolutely ordinary routines that consume our hours on the blue planet. A good laugh is, as *Reader's Digest* has long pointed out, the best medicine for us all.

Consider the jokes that make the rounds in most organizations. There are jokes attacking the innocence of women and the intelligence of various ethnic and minority groups. There are jokes about malfunctioning body parts and misplayed sex, wise cracks about what it takes to make it here and those who have done well despite themselves. There are a few jokes about successful bosses and fisherman, but a great many more about the boss who was outsmarted or the big ones that got away. No one jokes about happy marriages or rewarding relationships, but they do joke about henpecked husbands and nagging or nymphomaniac wives. There are virtually no jokes about tall, handsome persons, but a barrage of humor about short, fat, bald, ugly ones, ranging from self-depreciating and harmless to malicious and spiteful. In short, our jokes tend to be about things or persons we mistrust, fear, don't understand, or simply hate.

By telling a joke we *transcend* or rise above our ordinariness, commanding the attention of those present, entertaining them by our quick, laudible performance, gaining the reward of their laughter or false disgust. For a moment we are famous, and the feeling of that moment can help us through the rest of the day, sometimes the rest of a week. If the joke is a really good one it will get around, and there we will be, listening to someone else tell "our" joke back to us, rewarding us again by imitating what we have done so well. To be a person who "cannot tell a joke" is, in organizational America, a source of weakness, something that needs to be admitted up front, a flaw requiring a public apology, something we ought to overcome.[2] Probably the only thing worse than not being able to tell a joke is not allowing yourself to laugh at one. For then, you are truly a social wimp, a miscreant, a humorless person.

There are practical and social problems associated with company humor. The problem is not the jokes themselves, but what they *imply* about the joketeller or the assembled crowd. For example, within some organizational cultures, some kinds of jokes are not tolerated because they are seen as reflections of personal attitudes or values. When these attitudes or values are negatively directed toward a particular social class, ethnic group, or race, those who laugh are seen as identifying with the attitude or value. You don't simply laugh at the humor in the story, you laugh because it *really* reveals what you believe. Unfortunately, because most of our humor is directed at the misfortunes of others, or stereotypes based on ethnic, racial, or sexual identities, there aren't many jokes to tell if you can't tell "those" jokes. You are situationally reduced to word plays and puns, or "safe" stories, which are seldom as funny or rewarding as the dirtier, meaner varieties.

Most humor is dirty and mean. For example, most of *us* (fill in whatever group you belong to) don't understand or empathize easily with *them* (fill in all other racial, ethnic, or sexual groups), unless there happens to be one of "them" who married into our family or present for the joke. When "they" talk in their own language, we think they know something we don't know or they are making fun of us. Sometimes we think "they" are sexually better equipped than "we" are, sometimes we think "they" have more money or power than "we" do (and if all was right in Eden, of course, "we" would have the money and the power), and sometimes we fear their physical, mental, or professional strength. We don't like competing with them and we don't understand or empathize with them well enough to cooperate successfully with them, so we discriminate against them in jokes, stories, and in the laughter we supply to others' jokes and stories about them. The minorities we joke about usually don't like the fact that they con-

[2]The exception to this rule may be found among employees of the United States government, for whom, as one of our reviewers pointed out, a sense of humor may be considered a character flaw, a sign that one isn't a serious person.

stantly overhear how many of them it takes to change a lightbulb from us, so they invent their own jokes about us, told in their inner circles. In addition to being rude, humor about minority groups can also be inconvenient. A joke can create suspicion between peers, drive a wedge of permanent embarrassment between persons. How jokes operate in your organization is a very serious issue.

Listen to the jokes told around you in the workplace *before* you tell one. You need to know what the standards for humor are before you accidentally say something you will later regret. Avoid laughing at jokes told about persons in the organization until you get to know them. Be especially careful when jokes are told about the boss because chances are the boss doesn't like being the butt of company humor. The best policy for newcomers to any organization seems to be to joke about persons and things that can't hurt you. Joke about the machinery, the computer, the abstract rules, the transportation system, political figures, or even yourself. Joke about the abstract, not the specific. Make Murphy your patron saint of humor, and remember that Murphy's Laws also include the following laws of organizational humor:

—You never see the Chairman of the Board until you tell a joke about her or him.
—Practical jokes keep liability lawyers in business.
—The only good time to joke with the boss is at the exit interview.
—The meaning of any joke is in the mind of its hearer, who may not like you very much.

While there is nothing that lifts the spirit from the gray everydayness of working so much as a properly sarcastic remark or deliciously dirty dig, these sources of humor should always be confined to those persons whom you completely trust. Remember, dear old Socrates had something wise to say about everyone and everything, and he wound up getting poisoned by his peers.

On Storytelling

Ever since we listened to our first story, probably while resting on Mommy or Daddy's knees, we have learned to appreciate storytelling. Stories are rich sources of cultural information, myths, legends, and lies, and though they mask themselves as anecdotes, fables, and reminiscences, they are vital to any real understanding of an organization's history and beliefs.[3]

You will hear three distinct kinds of stories in organizations.[4] Individuals will often relate stories about themselves, including isolation of events in which they were able to rise to the leadership demands of an imposing situation, or overcome an earlier defeat, or display one-upsmanship.

Individuals will also tell collegial stories about their co-workers, usually in the guise of "how things *really* are around here," or mythic accounts of heroes and heroines who saved the company from ruin by finding the Xerox key or by stalling a client on the phone. Collegial stories cover a wide range of human experiences, and are as often humorous as they are serious.

Corporate stories, however, tend to almost always be very serious, and through them we hear the philosophies and ideologies of "us" and "them," as well as legends of how we outsmarted the competition, met an impossible deadline, or contributed significant amounts of money to the poor. These stories tend to *symbolize* the consciousness of the organization, point to its defining characteristics, and thus encourage us, as individual corporate employees, to *identify* our ways with the company's.[5]

Stories are important sources of information. Stories that are repeated can become legends, myths, or company policy. They are

[3]See I.I. Mitroff and R.H. Kilmann, "Stories Managers Tell: A New Tool for Organizational Problem-Solving," *Management Review*, 64 (1975), 19–20; see also J. Marshall and R. Stewart, "Managers' Job Perceptions. Part I; Their Overall Frameworks and Working Strategies," *Journal of Management Studies*, 16 (1981), 177–190, and M.E. Pacanowsky and N. O'Donnell-Trujillo, "Organizational Communication as Cultural Performance," *Communication Monographs*, 50 (1983), 126–147.

[4]See M. E. Pacanowsky and N. O'Donnell-Trujillo, *op. cit.*, pp. 138–139.

[5]The concept of identification as a persuasive mechanism can be found in the works of Kenneth Burke, see especially his *A Rhetoric of Motives* (Berkeley, Cal.: University of California Press, 1969). For an example of how identification works to limit decision making, see G. Cheney, "The Rhetoric of Identification and the Study of Organizational Communication," *The Quarterly Journal of Speech*, 69 (1983), 143–159.

repeated because they are meaningful, and even if the meaning is limited to a particular person or group, the story can reveal biases, prejudices, ways of knowing, and goals that can become important to you as you deal with the storyteller. Now that we have examined humor and storytelling in organizations, let's take a close look at how to find the prevailing cultural wisdom.

CULTURAL WISDON: LEARNING THE ROPES

We emphasize the dual demands of professional and social skills in any organization. A major part of developing social skills that can help you rise on the corporate grease pole is maintaining friendly contacts with others. Through friendly contact we learn the rules and roles of appropriate company behavior, the history of the organization and its members, and acquire guides to executive performances that we can master. We may also make a friend or two; but remember, it is best to develop organizational friendships *slowly* because sudden changes in the company climate can spell disaster between or among friends. How do you learn whom to trust?

The answer is you have to be carefully taught. The internal radar we discussed earlier is not available at your local electronics store. Even if you come well equipped with it from your last position, you will need to fine tune your communicative social style to the blips and beeps of the new environment. Essentially this means you need to locate a good consultant by following a few simple rules.

1. *The people who greet you first are usually the ones who need you the most.* Be careful of the friendly approachers who encroach on your private space and drape an all-too-friendly arm over your shoulder. These folks may be nice persons, but their niceness may be entirely strategic—they may need you more than you need the advice you can get from them. Disgruntled employees searching for uninformed allies, lonely persons needing encouragement, persons trying to collect admirers, followers, or friends, and the occasional weirdo whom no one else will talk to may approach you

for the purpose of taking you in. In any organization, you are guilty until proven innocent, guilty by association, and just plain potentially guilty most of the time. To associate with the company dregs is to lower yourself; to follow their advice is to lower yourself completely. Remember: Every social relationship is based on an assumed *exchange*. You need to figure out what the other person is getting out of being with you before you follow any "free" advice.

2. *People who unnecessarily self-disclose are looking for details about you, or are weak themselves.* Be very careful around people who tell you more about themselves than you want to know. Be suspicious of others who ask you questions that are illegal under Title VII (e.g., questions about your personal and family life, your friends and enemies, your marital status and general state of happiness, etc.). If you get to know too much about someone, you may feel more responsible for them than you need to, and when someone finds out *your* personal secrets or fears, they have an incredibly powerful hold over you. Of course you can't just walk around giving your name, rank, and telephone number. You need to discuss the news, weather, and sports, exchange movie and record reviews, concert and civic information, and gossip *only* about restaurants. Run for cover when friendly talk turns intensely personal, and you are indelicately asked for information about your income, love life, illnesses, or anything usually reserved for your mother, analyst, or bartender.

3. *Be suspicious when money issues are raised.* There are always people around who are not doing well financially. This problem has been compounded in recent years by inflation, because it is common for a person with 15 years of experience to be earning less than the newcomer with an MBA. They may ask you directly how much you earn to acquire yet another bitch about how the company treats them, in which case they will most certainly use your name in vain. Or they may openly reveal how much they are making and wait for you to reciprocate. In either case, a fool and information about his or her income are soon parted. Another scheme worthy of some detail is the con. Some persons try to borrow money from newcomers because others in the organization have learned they won't pay it back. You can get nickled and

dimed (these days quartered and possibly drawn) to death by people who just don't have the right change for the coffee machine or who fumble slowly at the bar while waiting for the commuter train. Here are some of the more subtle social strategies of the con that can leave you penniless:

> Oh, oh. I didn't realize how late it was. Get this check, will you, I've got to dash or I'll miss my train. I'll get the next round next time. . . . (There may never be a next time, or a next round. A free round a day can add up to more than $200 a year, depending on prices.)

> I'm out of change. Get this cup of coffee, will you? (Some people make it a point never to carry change. A free cup of coffee once in a while adds up to about $100 a year pure profit for the mooch.)

> If you are going to the bakery, don't forget to pick up a donut for me. (Once you hand over the donut, money will seldom be mentioned. After all, the person didn't say "loan me the money for a donut," so he or she takes it as a gift. A free donut a day also adds up to more money than you typically spend on a nice gift for your parents once a year!)

> I forgot my wallet. Lend me five bucks so I can buy my train ticket." (This parlay cannot be played every day, but it is possible to make $200 to $500 a year on ticket loans not paid back.)

These examples show how a clever mooch can earn up to $700 a year extra income. This amount could cover a brief summer vacation in Martinique, or a nice skiing trip in the mountains, complete with rental of gear. Too bad you won't be able to go because the money somehow just seems to disappear. . . .

A really clever moocher in a large company with reasonable turnover can get two drinks ($4), three cups of coffee ($1.20), two donuts ($.50), and a $5 train ticket each day, for a total of $12.70 per day, or $63.50 a week. This adds up to a grand, tax-free total of $3,175 for a 50 week year (two weeks off on that vacation you paid for).

The rule of thumb is: If you get hit twice with no return, avoid that person forever. If you really want to get even, you could type out a bill and present it to the mooch in public, saying "You owe me two donuts, three cups of coffee, and a train ticket, but I'll take $7.00 in cash." Be especially careful of lunchtime behavior. If you take a check once and fail to get the person to pay for the next one, it may set a pattern. Keep in mind, also, that it is very annoying to lunch with the meticulous types who use pocket calculators to divvy up the check:

> Now, let's see. Susan had the reuben and slaw with coffee, or did you have tea? Tea. That's $4.50. Bill had the chicken salad and iced tea, so that's $2.50, and Bernice had the knackwurst and beer for $3.85. With tip, that's, let's see, 5 plus 3 plus 5 at 20% with mine on too, is about 20, so that's $4.00 and the tax. Susan, yours comes to $6.50, Bill is four bucks, and Bernice is $5.50. I'll put it on my credit card and you guys can just pay me. I need the cash for train fare.

If you paid attention you could see the check actually came to $14.85 plus $.75 tax. With a 15% tip, the whole lunch is $17.50. The meticulous calculating mooch has collected $16.00. So his meal costs $1.50, plus he puts it on his credit card, calls it a business lunch and takes a 30% tax deduction. He gets back $5.25, for a net luncheon profit of $3.75 plus lunch! Who says there is no such thing as a "free lunch" these days!!

4. *Find a mentor and a productive network.* The best way to acquire the necessary social skills, contacts, and corporate wisdom is to find a mentor and a productive network. There are always old veterans in any organization who want some connection with the future. They do this by adopting some young sprout who appeals to them and the exchange basis of the relationship goes like this: you need my wisdom, I need your youthful acceptance. Together we can do better than either one of us can do alone.

There is no good way to make it entirely on your own. There are an incredibly large number of talented, purposeful, energetic beings in every company. The ones who advance their careers usually have help from reliable vets, and the ones who make it all the way to the corner office at the top always do. The issue of *who you know* versus *what you know* is easily resolved. What you know gets you the job and helps you keep it. Who you know pushes you ahead of the competition and supports you in times of crisis. There is no way to make it without adequate social support any more than you can make it if you are uninformed and incompetent.

We are not advising you to be a "brown noser." You can be an effective courtier without appearing to be a lackey simply by locating persons you can genuinely respect and demonstrating to them you are also worthy of respect. A smart old-timer can easily recognize sycophantry anyway. But it is important to powerful persons to have nice folks around them who understand and respect their power.

If this advice sounds medieval, it is. But experienced heads can provide the information you need to advance. They can also call attention to the swell job you are doing. They run interference for you and mention your name when it counts. They can keep others off your back and tip you off to emerging opportunities ahead of the public announcement. For your part, your respect and attention make them look good. You also provide them with information they could not otherwise receive—what is happening among the "younger" folks in the company, who can be trusted, who has brains, who is an enemy.

However rosy a portrait we paint about mentors and networks, we must concede that women seldom fare as well in their search for the wise old sage and social acceptance among the ranks of men. There are many reasons for this. First, some women do *fear* success.[6] They either believe they can't succeed because they lack influence, or they shouldn't succeed because they will fit too easily into the stereotyped bitchy female boss who has no legitimate male companions and is equally estranged from her female colleagues. A second reason is the general problem of sexual harrassment in the office.[7] Although most companies give lip service to sexual abuse, and even write formal guidelines for dealing with the offenders, the issue of sexual harrassment is always an emotional one. And, despite their rhetoric to the contrary, most organizations

[6]See K. Deaux, "Internal Barriers," in J.J. Pilotta (Ed.), *Women in Organizations*, Prospect Heights, Ill.: Waveland Press, 1983, pp. 11–22.

[7]See T. S. Jones, "Sexual Harrassment in the Organization," in J.J. Pilotta (Ed.), *Women in Organizations*, pp. 23–38.

would prefer to lose the low-ranking female than the high-ranking male, even if he is the aggressor. Women are burdened by the desire, the demand, to be physically attractive, and yet not call "undue attention" to their secondary sexual characteristics. They are too often seen as potential sexual conquests rather than talented professional persons by older males who will exploit them, if given the opportunity to do so. As many recent public cases demonstrate, the younger female who does exchange sexual favors with older executives risks everything to gain very little. The hostility from other employees, the rumors, the gossip, the possible breakup of families, and the ruinous effect on a career don't seem to be worth the momentary act of passion which all too soon turns into regret.

Women have formed networks to deal with the problem of making productive contacts in any organization or profession. The result has been less effective than the idea, primarily because women who form networks generally exclude men who could help them, and thus further separate themselves from the existing power structures. A second reason for network demise is that professional networks require careful goal and agenda setting if they are to be productive. Unfortunately, most early networks were little more than lists of phone numbers or occasional social events that did not attempt to accomplish specific objectives. More recent attempts appear promising, but only if the network is able to integrate task and social functions, and include males.[8]

5. *Make sure the person giving you advice knows what she or he is talking about.* Every organization is analogous to a *community*, and authorities on communities believe that to identify power you need to find persons who understand who says what to whom with influence, and figure out why they are willing to talk to you about it. You have to be able to separate information from rumor, truth from gossip, informed opinion from idle talk. One of the best guides to finding a reliable source is to look for someone who is successful in the organization. If the person giving you free advice

[8]See S. DeWine, "Breakthrough: Making It Happen with Women's Networks," in J.J. Pilotta (Ed.), *Women in Organizations*, pp. 85–101.

doesn't look like he or she is making it, chances are the advice isn't worth listening to.

Consider the following propositions about identifying good advice and advice-givers:

1. There are always persons who know the truth. Sometimes, they will tell you about it. When you hear predictions from anyone, check out the results. Don't just pay attention to the times they were right—keep a won/lost record.

2. Most people really do not know how important company decisions are made, much less by whom, when, or even what the decisions are. Business is commonly conducted informally—in the bar, in the bathroom, at the club, in the lunchroom, at the restaurant. When deciders are ready to decide they decide, and they are responsible *only* to the persons who pay them and can fire them.

3. There is at least as much *disinformation* as information in any organization. Some managers purposefully start rumors to see who will later report it back to them. Sometimes decision makers "leak" almost accurate information to acquire support for a plan, or to see who supports a position they plan to reject. Not everything that comes down the grapevine is real, nor is it illusion—often it is both real and illusion simultaneously.

4. The organization chart is not necessarily an accurate guide to who has power or who makes decisions. Informal, socially based networks often control more information than formal chains of command.

5. You can acquire reliable information by being respectful of subordinates. For example, if you consistently treat secretaries or word processing operators with courtesy and genuine interest and appreciation for their jobs, you can find out what they know, which may surprise you. A good secretary rarely tells important secrets, and a secretary who acts as if she is divulging important secrets is probably giving disinformation.

6. Play an open hand if you want to acquire useful information from others. Do not divulge others' secrets, not ask others to

guard yours if you don't think they will do so. Treat everyone with courtesy and respect in public, and avoid gossiping about them in private.

Listening to the wisdom of sages, and making useful professional and social connections, are important organizational skills. To be good at them, you must become a reliable observer of human behavior before you make important decisions and commitments. Listening and observing require time and effort, both of which will be in short supply unless you also acquire the essential skills of organizing and strategic planning.

SOCIAL ORGANIZING: THE ART OF STRATEGIC PLANNING

The wisdom of the olden days was simple: Don't make friends at work, concentrate on doing your job, and do only one thing at a time. It isn't clear whether or not this advice worked in the olden days, but as they say in California, "for sure it wouldn't work like now, ya know?"

The world has turned around a good bit since behaving yourself meant minding your own business, avoiding getting to know people at work very well, and (we repeat) doing only one thing at a time. These days if you mind your own business you will be seen as either a chronic reticent for whom social life is alien or just plain strange. If you avoid getting to know people at work you will have a difficult time finding out what you need to know through informal channels of communication, and you will never become part of a productive network. And if you choose to do only one thing at a time chances are you will be perceived as a dunce who can *only* do one thing at a time. None of these descriptors fits the performance personality.

As we consistently point out in this book, you were hired to do a job, but your success in the organization depends as much on your social skills as it does on carrying out assigned tasks. The problem is organizations allot time for carrying out assignments but they do not allot time for social climbing.

You have to organize your time strategically if you are to accomplish the dual goals of professional and social acceptance. You should figure out what you need to accomplish each day, chart a way of completing each task in an efficient manner, and keep a record of how you are progressing throughout the workday. Of course you will have to respond to new contingencies as they occur, but *this should not deter you from meeting your daily objectives*.

You should have two basic goals to guide your daily planning. First, you must carry out the responsibilities you have been assigned. Regardless of how socially successful you are, you will get nowhere unless you can demonstrate competence on the job you were hired to do. Second, you should select a social agenda that includes "stopping by to say hi" to friendlies and making your network contacts. Limit your "stopping by" calls to a maximum of five minutes, and your network contacts to fifteen minutes. Now chart the route you must walk/drive to make these social calls. When and where do they overlap with your assigned duties? You should always be "on your way" to somewhere directly associated with your job when you stop to chat to exchange information. Nobody appreciates someone who simply goofs off on the job, which is usually defined as walking around doing nothing, or spending most of your time interrupting others from their work.

Phone calls are problematic. For many persons the phone is an intruder. It invades your privacy because it always seems to ring when you don't need or want it to ring. Simply calling people for the sake of making contact will be seen as a waste of time; furthermore, you may be butting in on someone who really needs the time. If this annoying habit continues, you may find yourself being put on endless hold, or being intercepted by a secretary who has been instructed to prevent your call from going through.

We are *not* encouraging you to make needless small talk a major part of your day. Small talk is generally for small persons, or for mindless conversations with strangers while both of you wait for someone else to rescue you. Babbling about Jim's middle name, or the color of the new car you plan to purchase, or how the local sports' teams are doing is usually self-destructive talk. The more you engage in it for its own sake, the more likely it will destroy you. Instead we recommend *purposeful, productive* social talk designed to acquire useful information, persuade someone who needs persuading, improve your image, or demonstrate your performative skills. Talk is not cheap unless the topics you choose to talk about are unimportant. You want people to be glad to see you, not because you can interrupt their work, but because talking to you will be a rewarding experience.

To make social talk a rewarding experience requires strategic planning. The general rule is: Talk should be adapted to the *needs and expectations* of the listener. Notice we do not advocate talk to "express yourself," nor do we advocate talking for the sole purpose of advancing your own ideas. If you walk around expressing yourself and your opinions, you will be seen as a conceited, self-centered, insensitive person. Unfortunately, this is exactly what most persons do. Instead of trying to adapt what they want to say to the needs and expectations of their listeners, they talk about the "wonderful world of me."

To become a more successful conversationalist is not as difficult as you might imagine. Good conversationalists begin with three basic understandings: (1) talk should be purposeful rather than spontaneous, (2) talk should be adapted to the needs and expectations of listeners, and (3) talk should conform to the general rules for social etiquette (e.g., learn to take turns rather than dominate the conversation, avoid discussing religion, politics, or deeply intimate subjects, and realize that part of any successful conversation is *play*—the ability to be entertaining and let others know they are entertaining you).

From these three basic understandings, good conversationalists develop *repertoires* of stories, anecdotes, jokes, and general concerns to use when the immediate situation does not suggest a natural topic to pursue. It is important to be able to discuss a wide variety of issues, from science to literature, from the stock market to fashion trends, from places to eat to places to go for a memorable vacation. In Chapter Five we provide our guide to becoming a successful snob, which, to a large extent, demands you become able to hold intelligent conversations. For now, though, we only want to point out the need to make your conversation fresh and well informed. The boring conversationalist is the person who only knows how to talk about work or his or her one special interest, and this is the sort of person any organization can do without.

How can you strategically plan for social encounters and conversations? First, organize your day. If you have a good idea of where you will be going and who you will be talking to, you can plan what you want to say on your way there. Remember, you don't need to talk about everything you know each time you open your mouth. You generally only bring up one subject during any social encounter. Thinking of one interesting thing to say shouldn't be difficult if you maintain hobbies, interests, and activities that are *also shared by your listeners*. If you can't think of anything interesting to say, you can always ask a question. The novelist and linguist Walker Percy rightly points out that humans typically only do two things with talk—make statements or ask questions—and the latter is always the safer strategy if you don't know how the former will be received.

The second component of strategic conversational competency is to make talking to you a pleasant experience. This is most easily accomplished by being as concerned about others as you are about yourself, and demonstrating this fact by adapting your choices of topics to your listener's interests. This way you not only acquire as much information about them as they acquire about you, but more importantly, you will always know how to end a conversation—you both have work to do. In this way, you contribute to a mutual sense of equity and respect for priorities.

Social organizing and strategic planning for social talk are vital to your personal and professional image. Acquiring these skills will contribute to the delicate, busy balance of your organizational career by proving you are capable of performing your assigned duties, performing your social obligations, and integrating the performances as only a person worthy of the label "professional" must.

Improving Your Social I.Q.

1. What constitutes social acceptance? How do you know when you are socially accepted? How important is the ability to make good conversation in determining social acceptance? If it is so important, why don't you spend more time improving your conversational skills?

2. Can you tell at least five good jokes without relying on racist, sexist, or ethnic slurs, or without being reduced to dead baby or old elephant jokes? Why not? Don't you think having a sense of humor is an important aspect of social acceptance?

3. We say you need to adapt your social talk to the needs and expectations of your listeners. How can you learn what their needs and expectations are? Do you think learning how to ask questions might help? What questions would you have to learn to ask?

THE SECRETS OF TIME AND SPACE MANAGEMENT

Time and space are more than concepts to inform physicists; they are real components of the performance personality. Time is the constant agony, the ticking away of life's opportunities while we wait for something to happen, wait to see someone to make something happen, or just wait to see. Time is never, contrary to the Rolling Stones' lyrics, on our side.

Space is different. Space waits to be organized, arranged, managed. Space exists to be made crowded, cramped, noisy, and foul, or pleasant, spacious, and airy. For many aspiring executives, space is, true to John Kennedy's dictum, the last frontier.

Time and space management are important because they form the background for your performances. They aid in the comprehension of meaning, co-contribute to the realities you shape and respond to. If you have control over them, you will inevitably have control over yourself and influence over others. Left unmanaged, they will control you, bending your behavior to suit their purposes, and always, always, leave you looking stressed to the point of weakness, disorganized to the point of confusion, and occasionally foolish.

There is irony in the message "an uncluttered desk is the sign of a sick mind," particularly acute when it oversees a cluttered desk and a harried, shattered person trying to locate a memo under piles of documents, articles of clothing, and old coffee cups. There is further irony in the statement "hurry up and wait, just like the military," spoken by a sweaty person who remained in the military for 20 years. In both cases, the symbolic utterances are saddening because they reveal a life somewhat out of control, and a person who cannot seem to take charge of it. They bespeak a quiet desperation and a stressed existence, but moreover they tell the story of persons who refuse to command their uses of time and space, maybe because they feel they can't—these are the gladly suffering victims of organizational dramas, the persons who complain about the mess their lives are in without recognizing they have chosen the mess. These are the slow losers, the persons who age badly and usually die young, who are passed over for promotions despite their competent work, who create a kind of cartoon shabbiness about themselves and are consistently punished because of it.

Organizations are built on the ideal of order, not chaos. Management is a concept based on the assumption that order can be created in the workplace, and when it has been created, the organization will run more smoothly because of it. Order is a kind of discipline, the same kind of discipline that contributes to good health, accomplishment of goals, and peace of mind. In each case, you are required to assume immediate responsibility for your own existence, to plan for the objectives you specify as desirable, and to work toward their accomplishment in a systematic, graceful, even eloquent way. Of course you will have to respond to urgent contingencies, momentary panics, and genuine human dilemmas, but these are the exceptions to the rule of routines, to the habits of organization and control.

These are the reasons why we call time and space management "secrets." They seem to be secrets to those who don't make use of them, who wonder outloud how so-and-so can find the time to do X, the space to contain all of Y. And for those few fortunate individuals who discover how to manage time and space in the human workplace, order and discipline seem so natural as to suggest the mastery of a fundamental truth.

An Organized Work Space is the Sign
Of a Comfortable Body and a Disciplined Mind

Most successful organizations grow faster than their acquisitions of space. It is not uncommon to see temporary partitions separating what should be real offices, nor is it unusual to hear people complain because they lack file space, terminal space, or a place to hang their hats and coats. A comfortable work space in a overcrowded environment is a feat in itself, a sign of the managerial spirit and a truly creative imagination. Remember, as odd as it is, people do use their general impressions about your *office* to inform their understanding of *you*. If it is a habitat fit only for meatblossoms and silent screaming, what does that signal about you?

Generally, work space is a power perk. Bonuses are sometimes paid in cash, sometimes in ambience. In most companies, you can figure out who is more important than whom by looking at the quality of desks, floor spaces, carpeting, and so forth. The U.S. Government only provides wooden executive desks and comfortable chairs for GS 15's and above—the rest get the standard gun metal gray symbols of ultimate averageness.

However your organization apportions workspace, you need to utilize what is given to you appropriately. Your space should always be neat, clean, free of clutter, and available for working. Files should be filed in file cabinets and drawers in the desk, not strewn around the room like disenchanted cheerleaders waiting for the bad ending to an awful game. Paperwork of any kind belongs in a file with an appropriate label attached to it for easy reference. These days most modern offices are making considerable use of computers, and if you can arrange to have a terminal in your office, you can organize your workspace much more efficiently. Don't say you are afraid of the keyboard, or staring at the screen will eventually blind you, or that you can't do math. Computer literacy is an absolutely essential skill of making it in any organization, and if you act like a pantywaist when the opportunity to make use of one arises, you will surely someday lose your job to someone else. In fact, modern office systems make it virtually certain that whole levels of middle managers will be replaced by direct computer access to data for decision making. The only middle managers who survive the invasion of the green screens will be those with their fingers already attached to the keyboards.

The basic rule for organizing your workspace is convenience. Everything you regularly use should be readily reachable—the phone, the terminal, the felt-tipped pen caddy, and notepaper, particularly memo pads. Quick reference lists of phone numbers can be taped to the inside of your top desk drawer (which otherwise only becomes a nesting place for dried-up pens, broken pencils, and trash), and a calendar should be within easy eye contact. If you can attach a phone answering device to your company extension, you gain a strategic advantage over your use of time. If you can install a rheostat for the lighting in your office you gain an important feature of the controlled office environment, which will be easier on your eyes and gentle on your mind.

The second rule of office organization is your personal comfort. No one works well when cramped, and finding a way to reduce the tension your body builds up during the day can be a genuine lifesafer. Your chair should be as firm as a recarro seat in a fancy Camaro, and as well constructed as the lumbar supports systems in a Volvo. If possible it should recline and swivel, and be situated on quiet rollers. If your office is carpeted, and you have any choice in the matter, choose soothing colors and foam backing to help drown out unwanted noise. You can always install a plastic mat so the rollers on your desk chair won't cut permanent imprints on the carpet, or fight you every move you try to make. Try to arrange your desk, chair, and files so that you have space to stand up, stretch out, do a few exercises, and pace comfortably. Tastefully add personal touches such as framed prints or portraits as you see fit, but remember everything in your office communicates to others what they want to see in it. The nice abstract impressionist nude is open to a variety of interpretations denied by a simple scene of the winter streets of the city blanketed in snow.

The third rule of office organization is communicative effectiveness. Where you place the visitor's chairs and how you organize the conference table do matter. If you choose to be separated from your visitors by your desk, then you encourage them to respect your authority but doubt your openness. If you can find a round conference table you will go a long way toward improving the feeling of equity and quality of discussions that go on around it. If you can remind yourself to move from behind your desk to a position of nonverbal neutrality while conducting interviews or informal discussions, you will communicate your understanding of the visual and spacial influences on human interaction.

These three rules of space management should not be seen as terciary considerations, things to do after you get your work completed. They are logical concommitants to getting your work done, and as such should command a high priority for the few minutes or even hours it takes to do it right.

SOME OTHER HIGHLY ESSENTIAL SKILLS

In this section, we offer a series of brief "ought tos." There are few "how tos" for most of these capabilities, but you "ought to" know how important they are and figure out ways to monitor your reactions to them. For the performance personality, these issues form vital pathways to reach personal and organizational objectives.

Handling Emergencies

For many persons, handling emergencies follows Murphy's motto: "When in trouble, when in doubt, run in circles, scream and shout!" For those persons who do not respond emotionally to emergencies, who prefer to keep a cool and even demeanor in the face of absolute disorder, there is a paraphrase to Kipling that aptly applies: "If you can keep your head while those about you are losing theirs and blaming it on you, then you simply do not understand the situation."

An emergency *is* an emotional situation. In most organizations, the common response to an emergency is to panic, look for the boss, and then complain loudly enough to distract attention from the real problem. This is a common response because it protects you against becoming suddenly accountable for the situation. You are merely, to borrow a line from a Kurt Vonnegut, Jr., novel, "the canary in the cage," announcing the disaster but not responsible for doing anything about it. The major problem is that the person who does take action to handle the emergency will also have to take the blame if something goes wrong. And the pressure of this simple thought on *your* mind is paralyzing. Suddenly you can't just "do something." Everything you do could turn out wrong, and your job might be the cost of it.

We advocate taking responsible action in any emergency. First, despite your feelings to the contrary, anything you do will be instantly appreciated by everyone else who only stands and stares. Second, you will be demonstrating leadership ability under fire—a talent most leaders really don't possess (probably including your boss). And third, blame can be apportioned later, after the situation is under control. You ought to handle emergencies.

Apportioning Rewards Among Subordinates

One of the principle causes of organizational demise—the kind which create emergencies—is the inability of a manager or supervisor to *equitably* apportion resources, pay, and work loads among subordinates. This is the case because we all operate under an assumed system of fairness—a kind of organizational golden rule—which rewards those persons who contribute to equity and punishes those who don't. As long as everyone behaves this way (which is almost never the case), the organization should run as smoothly as a well-oiled machine, and there should be happiness in the office.

The problem is organizations are slow to change. Most companies use semi-annual or annual performance reviews to make adjustments in pay, rank, resources, and objectives, so the everyday contingencies that alter assigned priorities, or cause imbalances to exist, seldom are addressed. Managers are supposed to monitor the situations they manage, but it is hard to think of equity when trying desperately to meet a deadline, or complete a major report. The busyness of doing business gets in the way of being fair.

We aren't providing excuses for managers who treat employees inequitably, but we do realize the magnitude of the problem. As a manager, you ought to keep a finger on the pulse. You ought to monitor who is getting and who is giving something up, and keep accurate documentation about resources and shortages. You ought to try to reward the virtuous and punish the harmdoing naysayers, and carefully define task objectives. You ought to know which of your field generals requires an army (or else she or he will try to gain control of your own), and which of them requires only an occasional kind word. And above all else, you ought to understand that money is always important—the person who worked very hard and received only an average increase in salary is likely to hold it against you. Find some other way to reward him or her, such as decreasing the busy work or increasing the status.

Working on Committees

Committees are a fact of life in organizations. For one thing, most problems and decisions are so complicated it takes more than one or two persons to handle them. Even more importantly, different groups have different stakes in solutions, and it is important to have everyone who might be affected by a decision participate in its creation.

The best way to understand committee or small group work is to understand the importance of agendas to guide discussion.[9] Make sure you understand the *process* guiding the decision-making or problem-solving enterprise. Most American organizations base agendas on three interrelated principles:

1. *Standard operating procedures* are the best way to guarantee that everything needing to be accomplished will be done. Most procedures are derived from either John Dewey's steps in reflective thinking (i.e., Standard Agenda, PERT, CPM), or the Rand Corporation's brainchild called "brainstorming" (i.e., Delphi technique, Brainwriting, Nominal Group Technique, etc.). A procedure establishes a systematic agenda for accomplishing the task and usually guides individual steps in the process.

2. *Individual contributions based on expertise or experience* encourage small group leaders to select group members from diverse backgrounds, each one with a reason for speaking. Recent evidence demonstrates the importance of making selection decisions based equally on expertise and personality, to ensure group members will adhere to agendas, and not overly concentrate on how much they dislike one another.

---

[9] See H.L. Goodall, Jr., *Small Group Communication in Organizations* (Dubuque, Iowa: William C. Brown, 1984), and G.M. Phillips, J.T. Wood, and D.J. Pedersen, *Group Discussion: A Practical Guide to Participation and Leadership*, 2nd ed. (New York: Harper & Row, 1984).

3. *Consensus as the goal of decision making* means everyone must agree on the final solution. Consensus can be achieved without taking a vote (which encourages us to think in terms of winners and losers), and productive conflict is natural to the process.

These three concomitants to agendas aid in the facilitation of effective discussion. However, individual group members are responsible for creating and adhering to the agendas once they are in place.

As a group leader, you ought to study agenda setting techniques and choose the ones most suited to the task at hand. You ought to carefully select group members based on experience with the problem, expertise, and personality. You ought to circulate a written agenda to all participants prior to the meeting, and make the first order of business any deletions or modifications in the agenda. You ought to introduce topics and then guide the discussion. You ought to help prevent destructive conflicts by planning against them and intervening directly when they begin to occur. You ought to ask everyone for input, and check every group member before announcing consensus. You ought to keep accurate records of each group meeting, and carefully document each individual's assignments and accomplishments (this is easier to do if you ask a secretary to sit in on discussions).

As a group member, you ought to prepare for discussions, and always arrive on time ready to engage in productive group communication. You ought to avoid hogging the floor, giving passionate speeches, and attacking the character or heritage of other group members. You ought to take notes when necessary, and complete all individual assignments on time. Above all else, maintain the human decency of the group (which is sometimes difficult if there are patent nitwits present), and avoid digressions (although they inevitably will occur).

Sustaining Your Professional Image

Being a "professional" only has the meaning your behavior has in the minds of others. In the broader context of professionalism, the term usually refers to acquiring a public reputation for informed opinions, solid reliability, honesty, and communicative competence. However admirable these goals are, they must be *observed* in the consistency of your actions and words if you are to become worthy of the heady label "a professional."

Maintaining a professional image is essential to success. The problem for most of us is not with the desire to be a professional, but with how that desire all too often conflicts with other desirable personal and social images. For example, we are encouraged by media to be physically attractive specimens, to dress according to prevailing fashion trends, and to become friends at work with members of both sexes equally. Very often these desirable personal images distract us from the business at hand. We want to be perceived as sexually desirable (who doesn't?), yet to attract attention to our sexuality is to court corporate trouble. We want to be perceived as fashionable without being trendy, but keeping up with fashion deters us from keeping up with financial statements or corporate reports that also demand scrutiny. We want to be friendly, but our attempts at friendship may be misperceived as sexual advances or attempts to form political alliances (which, in most cases, has some validity). Hence, the need to balance our personal and professional images is an ideal we usually can only hope to make progress toward, never fully embrace.

You ought to attain professional competencies before announcing that you are behaving like a professional. You ought to monitor how others are responding to your professional and personal images, and know when to separate or integrate the two. You ought to cultivate the difficult task of making claims about your knowledge and skills without seeming intolerably conceited or overly self-reliant. You ought to continue your professional education, and broaden your interests in the field of your choice. And you must always keep your options open—you can't be a professional if you don't have a job.

Dealing With the Boss

Most persons make two basic errors when dealing with the boss. First, they take up too much time discussing issues important only to them, rather than to the interests of the boss. Second, they avoid talking purposefully while they have the boss's ear. Both of these problems spell disaster.

The best advice we can provide is to make maximum use of the time you are allotted with the boss. When you have a good reason to talk to her or him, make an appointment, prepare your statement, and perform it brilliantly and efficiently. You want to be remembered as a productive, creative, reflective employee, not a time-wasting mooch who tells semi-amusing anecdotes and complains about the weather.

The second best advice we can provide is to know the difference between formal and informal communication channels, and between formal and informal communication. The former are more important when you are new on the job, because if you go over or around someone you usually make an enemy. Later, when you acquire a professional reputation and personal allies, you can make more frequent use of informal channels. But the second clause in the first sentence of this paragraph is always important. Too many persons ruin career opportunities by not recognizing the singular importance of differentiating between formal and informal talk. Don't try to make friends with the boss because chances are she or he already has established friendships more meaningful than any you could legitimately provide. Don't try to draw the boss into a political alliance; the boss will initiate those discussions with you at the appropriate time. And don't make promises or claims you can't keep or live up to because those will be the ones you are called upon to perform, by the boss.

So there you have it—the absolutely essential skills of making it in any organization. None of them alone will guarantee success, but you almost always need to acquire all of them to succeed. Sound difficult? Why do you think they call it *work*?

chapter four
THE PERFORMANCE PERSONALITY GOES TO WORK

"In modern social life adults must act narcissistically to act in accordance with society's norms."
—RICHARD SENNETT

"Watching out for yourself really means looking out for the other guy."
—THE AUTHORS

THE SINGULAR IMPORTANCE OF YEAR ONE

Physicans tell us that the first year of life is very important—if we survive it, our chances for making it to age six improve dramatically. *How* we survive the first year is perhaps even more important, at least in terms of our later development and maturity. If we survive year one in a happy, robust, healthy state, we tend to make those characteristics a permanent part of our personalities. So the first twelve months of living do tend to mark us irrevocably for the remainder of our lives.

The preceding statement also applies to the first year of anyone's organizational career. If you manage to survive it with a sense of purpose, humor, and creativity, then you can build on these accomplishments in the years ahead. Furthermore, the goal of the first year is more than mere survival, it is the preservation of your mental, emotional, and physical health against the stresses of working life. The goal of the first year of any career is not just survival, but a feeling of well-being that makes survival tolerable.

Finding out how to survive and prosper during the first year of organizational life receives less attention than virtually any other organizational topic.[1] Although many authorities make obvious statements about "making a good first impression," or "getting off on the right foot," or "guarding your image and territory," we know precious little about *how* to accomplish these complex goals.

This chapter is addressed to those persons who want to do more in their first year's work than simply survive with a regular paycheck. The examples and testimonies we offer are drawn from the informal biographies given to us by persons whose names we promised we wouldn't reveal, but whose experiences are worthy of attention and study.

Before we begin to explore year one and you, we need to define why we believe year one is of vital importance to you. Let's start with the facts. First, we know 70% or so of persons working in organizations report being dissatisfied with their job. Most attribute a major portion of their dissatisfaction *not* to the job itself but to (a) unrealistic expectations of working life, (b) mismanaged interpersonal relations with co-workers, (c) mismanaged time and misused human resources, and (d) perceived lack of influence with superiors and subordinates.[2] Second, dissatisfaction at work negatively affects the general quality of personal and professional life. Despite individual differences, a pattern of dissatisfaction usually can be traced back to events occurring during the first year of organizational life. Furthermore, the webs of emotional and professional unrest spun during the first year tend to enmesh you in a

---

[1]One important exception to this lack of literature is M.R. Louis, "Surprise and Sense-Making: What Newcomers Experience In Entering Unfamiliar Organizational Settings," *Administrative Science Quarterly*, 25 (1980), 226–251.

[2]See H.L. Goodall, Jr., "The Status of Communication Studies In Organizational Contexts," *Communication Quarterly*, 33 (1984), and F.M. Jablin, "Superior-Subordinate Communication: State-of-the-Art," *Psychological Bulletin*, 86 (1979), 1201–1222.

frustrated sense of confusion, catch you in tragedies of your own design.

A bad first year can and very often does have dire consequences for an otherwise promising organizational career. Poor performance appraisals create feelings of inequity and potential failure, and make it harder to change jobs because of unfavorable recommendations. Ruined relations with co-workers are difficult to repair, and trying to do so interferes with work. And, of course, as personal distress rises our bodies and minds tend to become less reliable, less healthy, less efficient. Clearly the issues related to happiness and well-being during the first year of a career are important ones.

THE FIRST YEAR IN RETROSPECT: FOUR WAYS OF REMEMBERING IT FROM THE FABULOUSLY SUCCESSFUL TO THE MISERABLY FAILED . . .

PROFILE: The following case was taken from interviews with a young man who made a career within the broadcasting industry. He was born in West Virginia, reared in that part of that state's eastern panhandle known mostly for John Brown's raid and hanging, and educated at the regional four-year college located there. Since his early teens he has been involved in radio as a hobby and a profession. Graduation from college prompted him to seek a career as a high school teacher. He located a teaching position, spent five years instructing students in English, drama, speech, and journalism. He was paid according to the standard scale for high school teachers and found himself increasing his debts and diminishing the success of his marriage. These financial difficulties contributed to the collapse of his marriage when he was 25, and to his "retirement" from teaching at the age of 26. At that time, he was making less than $12,000 and was heavily in debt. He sold his automobile and home, and after dividing the profits with his ex-wife, he began a second career as a radio salesperson for a small Pennsylvania-based Top-40 station. Here is how he made it through his first year.

Jason H.

I thought crazy things during those first days and nights. I mean, I was still a young guy, and I knew I was smarter than most people my age. Anyway, I promised myself that I would make it, that I would break whatever sales records that station had and climb to the top of the business. It was a challenge I offered to me. And I took it seriously. In retrospect, I think I was more than a little bit driven.

Anyway, I did exactly what I set out to do during the next six months. I was putting in about 18 to 20 hours a day on the road, driving over a thousand miles a week making calls on businesses in a three-state region. I learned how to sell by selling, and my motivation for sales came from deep down inside. I was proving something to myself. Then a tragic thing happened. My boss, a guy in his early forties, dropped dead of a heart attack. This is the guy who had been kidding me about being a "workaholic," and yet he was doing about what I was doing every day. More than that, he was my friend, my mentor. He had given me a chance when nobody else would. Now he was dead. Poof, *gone*. The whole experience was too sudden, and not dramatic at all. I left the station one morning, he keeled over, and when I was told about it he was being dressed for the grave. The next thing I know is I inherit his job.

I started thinking—he was only about 15 years older than me when he died. Fifteen years. He used to tell me, over and over again, "if you haven't made it in this business by the time you're 30 or 35, you'll die young from the stress." He was exactly right, at least in his own case. So I figured I had about nine years left, if I took odds on the upper limit of his projection.

I *really* started working then. I hired two new saleswomen who were both good-looking, articulate, and persuasive. We changed the station's format to include some old R&B numbers blended with the Top-40 stuff. We changed our logo, and applied for an increase in operating power with the FCC. Sales were never better, and I was taking 15% of the total, including what my saleswomen were doing. I never had so much money in my life, although now it doesn't seem like so much. In fact, I went back to visit my old high school principal, the one I taught under and fought with for five long years, and thanked him for helping me leave. I told him that in less than one year

83

I had tripled my income and had learned how to enjoy living again. He still hated me.

Then it happened. There was a Washington, D.C. based network affiliate with an opening for a sales manager. This was a potentially first-class operation, only they had become almost invisible in their market. I would have 100,000 watts of FM to command, and a network connection to boot. I spent four days preparing for my interview, and devised one of the most outlandish plans ever invented. I knew this was going to be a once-in-a-lifetime opportunity, and I was ready for it. What I proposed was a General Manager's position that would include responsibility for sales and programming activities. That way I could finally do what I always wanted to be able to do—put a station on the air *my way*. I had drawn up plans for the format I was proposing—a crossover R&B/Soul mix with a whole new approach to airing spots and news. I borrowed an idea from a rock band album cover for a logo, and even prepared sample billboard and television promos for it. I talked nonstop for over three and one-half hours. The V.P. for Broadcasting from the network, all the senior station staff, and a couple of lawyers were in the room. I rehearsed this performance like a stageplay. I was great!

They bought the plan, lock, stock, and barrel. Deficit financing was arranged through the network to get us started. I asked for, and received, an initial salary of $50,000 plus stock options and 5% of the station's net profits during the first three operating years. Imagine that. Here I was, 27 years old, not quite one full year's experience in the field, and all of a sudden I am the CEO, more or less. I had successfully negotiated a salary over five times what I had been making the previous year! And I had power. I believed in God, America, and myself all at once.

I never felt so proud, nor so good, nor worked so hard in my life. For the next year or so I persuaded, pushed, shoved, prodded, coaxed, dealed, and intimidated my way to the goals I had established for the station. Within one year we captured a significant share of the market with a format we called "Disco-Radio," a format appealing to aspiring lower and middle-class blacks invented by a white, ex-high school teacher from West Virginia. I don't claim all the credit for my success, or the success of the format. My salespersonnel were the best. I even had a guy from the (Washington) Redskins working for me during the off-season. I treated all of them like brothers and sisters and we all made money, big money.

But I wasn't naive, either. I knew from studying the history of radio that what we had accomplished would last about three to five years, tops. Anything gets old when you play it again, and again, and again, Sam. So we milked it during the best of times, and set ourselves up for the split that would come during the worst of times.

The day I turned thirty I resigned from the station to assume a network vice-presidency. With the right investments I'm pretty much set for life. I have a new life, a new wife, and the self-respect that comes from knowing you've made it big in America on your own. And you know what? I still wake up nights sometimes and think about those days back during the beginning. What if I hadn't taken my mentor seriously? What if I had just walked through the motions of the job? What if I dreamed the American Dream without striving to make it come true? That first year meant a lot to me. Sure I had the breaks go my way, but I also worked very hard to make them go my way.

Jason's story spells SUCCESS, American style. However, it would be too easy to leave it at that. In his statement, there are several clues to how he made it to the top.

First, his motivation to succeed was based both on earlier failures and belief in his abilities, particularly his ability to learn. Many similar cases could be described. From the depths of personal despair only the strongest find within themselves the courage to turn their lives around. In Jason's case, he *needed to feel* successful, needed to prove (to his ex-wife? to his ex-boss? to his mother? to his friends? to himself?) he was worthy of respect. He was also willing to work very hard to attain his goals.

Second, he speaks carefully when describing his relationship with his mentor—the 40 year-old man who dropped dead of heart failure. To Jason, this man and the tragic event of his death is a very important memory—it attains a symbolic quality transcending ordinary experience or meaning. We are reminded of other success stories expressed in similar feelings about critical moments or episodes in a life: Scott Fitzgerald's failed courting of Zelda Sayre, which pushed him to write his first successful novel and in turn win her love; Lee Iacocca's failure at Ford Motor Company and later his incredible success at Chrysler; or the vision of IBM's founder, Thomas Watson, Sr., based on his association with men and women who worked in production assembly lines and sales.

Third, Jason used his knowledge of the broadcasting industry to guide his career choices. Here is a man who learned from a careful study of the past. Not content to ride on the glories of his youth, he planned career moves around new challenges and opportunities for growth. He moved from success in corporate responsibilities to autonomy, thus fulfilling a desire to accomplish self-sufficiency by the age of 35.

Finally, there is no doubt Jason is a very bright, creative, smooth person. He is a performance personality. He possesses a kind of charisma, a rhetorical charm, which he uses to further his business relationships. He uses his knowledge of literature to influence his sense of business, and sense of business to gain the loyalty of his staff. If he does well, they do well. Within this formula for success we see the creation of a professional network, a powerful, personal, task-oriented network of persons who want to share in the success that, as a coordinated team, they can create.

PROFILE: The following case is taken from conversations with a young woman who has reached a corporate vice-presidency at the tender age of 34. She was born in Washington, D.C., and reared in 11 different places, ranging from West Berlin, Germany, to San Diego, California, to Huntsville, Alabama. These moves were caused by her father's work with the United States Army. She grew up in a family best described as traditional and Protestant. She has four older brothers, and she is the only female child. She is attractive and well educated. She received a bachelor's degree in computer science and business administration from M.I.T. and earned her MBA from the Harvard Business School. She is fluent in six languages. Although she claims to lead an active social life, she has never been married and maintains no close associations with women or men. She claims to prefer the company of men, particularly older men. Her hobbies include flying, horseback riding, and playing the stock market.

Jacqueline V.

I don't usually indulge in self-disclosure or autobiography, as you call it. I grew up in a family that made a wonderful distinction between public and private life, and I maintain that point of view.

You asked me about my first year at —————. It was carefully planned. I was aware of the fact that the industry I chose to enter was dominated by men, and that being a woman was not necessarily an advantage. However, I grew up with four brothers and a very strong father. I knew how to deal with men on their own terms and I think that is very important.

Well, my first year was hectic. I remember being introduced to people all the time, being called "a bright young woman with a future here," and that kind of thing. I was cautious about the way I dressed, the way I talked, and the moves I initiated within the company. I had technical expertise in computer software and hardware, and worked very diligently to learn the intricacies of finance. During my first year, I was put in charge of a long-term project, the kind of project designed to keep you busy and out of the way. Instead of being resentful, I worked as long and as hard as I could to make this project the showpiece of the organization. I took some early risks that paid off. I knew I had one important show to do in six months' time, and that my performance would determine my next assignment. I hired a professional speechwriter to work on my presentational style, and I made use of the technology I had available to me to really stage a production for the brass—front and rear projection screens, computer-generated graphics, that sort of thing. The presentation took about an hour, and then I fielded questions for the next 40 minutes or so. Needless to say the show was a stunning success. My next assignment was a first-class opportunity, and I completed it two months ahead of schedule.

So much for the glamour. There is a darker side to this success story, which is more difficult to describe. We use small groups to generate all of our projects, and to make all of our decisions. I was, at least until recently, the only woman in the room. At first some of the men tried to put the moves on me, and to devalue my expertise by authority of their manhood. I deferred from both situations, of course. But I didn't ever embarrass any of them, nor did I openly accuse them of not playing straight with me. It took time, but slowly I won them over to my side. Now they say I'm just like "one of the guys," although I don't think that is an accurate description since I don't engage in the sort of locker-room verbiage they do. The point here is that I never came across as a "liberated" female or indulged in the mindless political discussions that characterize the conversations of many professional women. For this reason, other women in the organization don't care for me very much. They can't use our common bond of womanhood to advance their causes or their careers. And so many of them make political mistakes during their first year because of their pettiness that it haunts them forever.

I think the fact that I turned disadvantageous situations into opportunities to demonstrate my expertise is what made the difference in my career. Working is a long rehearsal for the few times you actually get a chance to show what you know, and if you perform well on those choice occasions you will inevitably succeed.

Jacqueline's testimony to success is both proud and frightening. Proud because she points to the performance nature of organizational work and because she has managed to work her way to a vice-presidency without sacrificing her character, body, or values. Her testimony is also frightening, however, because the words she speaks are noticeably cold, as if her obsession with success encouraged her to become manipulative and self-centered. She keeps her distance at all times. Unfortunately, this appears to be the price some women are willing to pay to achieve a sense of equity in organizations.[3]

Jacqueline's strategy for dealing with men is noteworthy, although certainly not unique. She claims to be just like "one of the guys" from their point of view, although she clearly rejects their interpretation. She seems to fit within an organization dominated by males by separating herself from the company of other women, and by avoiding open, public criticism of male sexual advances and innuendo (hence thwarting the advance without condoning it). Jacqueline does not speak of friends, mentors, or cronies. When you speak with her you get the distinct feeling that she is, by choice, a loner. Thus, she has succeeded in becoming a corporate success by creating an image of herself—as a Machiavellian—cool, manipulative, sensitive to the politics of the organization, unquestionable expertise combined with strongwomanship. Perhaps Oscar Wilde's nasty phrase best characterizes Jacqueline's image:

---

[3]See J. Koester, "The Machiavellian Princess: Rhetorical Dramas for Women Managers," *Communication Quarterly*, 30 (1982), 165–172.

"She hasn't got any enemies and her friends don't like her either." To build a dynasty of power by constructing walls instead of well-tempered bridges is to win the battle but have no one to share the victory with.

The preceding profiles documented the rise of persons who succeeded in their chosen fields, albeit at different costs and with vastly different strategies. The following two profiles tell less appealing stories. In the first case, we see how a young man snatched defeat from the jaws of victory, and in the second case we see how a young woman acquired a corporate reputation, but not the one she was aiming for.

PROFILE: The following case is developed from interviews conducted with Steve J., a Boston-based corporate lawyer with political aspirations. Although Steve is 33 and has attained success in the field of health/medical law, he still remembers his first year with a powerful firm as being the worst season of his life. Here, in his own words, is the story of a young man who had it all, and simply put, he blew it.

Steve was born in Denver and reared in the suburbs of Philadelphia. He graduated validictorian from a suburban high school, and won an honors scholarship to The University of Pennsylvania. At Penn, he studied history and political science, and acquired a minor in foreign languages (French and Russian). He graduated with high honors and went on to Yale University's School of Public Health, from which he emerged two years later with a M.P.H. degree in health administration. From Yale he traveled south to Washington, D.C., where he went through four years at Georgetown Law School while working full-time for a prominent health lobbyist. His formal education then completed, he diligently sought out the best possible first job. He sent out over 500 résumés to firms located in 20 states and three foreign countries. He spent nearly six months being interviewed, and was roundly regarded as one of the top prospects in his chosen field. Finally, after much lost sleep, he decided to join a prestigious firm whose home office is in Washington, D.C. There he was to work on a very important case involving the use of a fire-retarding substance in federal construction projects that had recently been linked to a variety of cancer-related deaths. Although he was not the principal lawyer on the case, he was given crucial research assignments. Here is the rest of the story.

Steve.

I was assigned to the ————— case because I was supposedly a health law specialist. After all, in fairness to the firm, that is what my résumé said. And it was, in part, consistent with my educational background and interests. However, getting a master's degree in health administration does not qualify anyone to be either a coroner nor a construction expert, and this case required more knowledge than I had. Probably it would have worked out—because I am good at legal research—but they thought I was such a fair-haired young man that they also assigned me the task of passing the bar exam in New York and California (Steve had already practiced law in Virginia).

I just didn't know how to say "no." I did, or tried to do, exactly what I was told. You have no idea how difficult it is to pass the New York or California bar exam—most good attorneys spend at least three to six months preparing for each one of them. So here I was trying to pass both of them within 30 days while doing very difficult research on the case.

It is very hard to tell you how I felt then. I was too ambitious for my own good, and being smart and well educated didn't make my life any easier. People want to take you to lunch, which takes time; show you off at their club, which takes time; do this, do that, and if you have any political savvy at all, you know you are supposed to be able to do all of these things well. So I went. Right down the tubes.

First, I flunked both bar exams. I don't think I even came close on the New York one. Then I botched a very important piece of research by not recalling a very simple statistical principle: You can't use correlations to make causal arguments. I did use a correlation for that purpose and ended up by arguing something about as dumb as the old rube about telephone poles and heart attacks both increasing since 1955, so obviously telephone pole construction *causes* heart attacks. I mean it was really dumb. I still think I made the mistake because I was depressed about not passing either of the exams. At that point, six or seven months into my first job, I was seriously doubting my abilities as a lawyer.

So then one day I was walking down a corridor in the office building and a door opened. It had been one of those closed-door meetings that weren't supposed to go on. Anyway, the long and short of it was that I was fired on the spot. No warnings, no sympathy, no severance pay. Just like that.

You see, my mistake on the research assignment was a sign to them that I was fallible. If you are supposed to be the "best and the brightest" in your field you aren't allowed to make mistakes, at least not mistakes like that one. And to add insult to injury, I had flunked the boards in both states where a good portion of my practice for them would take place. That was the ticket out. I'll never forget the expression on the old man's face when he broke it to me none too gently. He was actually outraged. He told me that as far as he was concerned, he had wasted seven months salary on a dunce. He also called me other names—fraud, bum, leper. He promised me that my legal career was over. If he could have thrown me out the door without straining his old bones past their limits I am convinced he would have. Nils Lofgren sings a song where he says "No mercy, no quarter, no place to hide from the other man." That was my feeling, exactly.

Now comes the truly sad part of the story. You try to get a job after being fired from one of the most prestigious law firms in the world. You try to get a job without references from your most recent employer. In the vast network that is the real world of corporate law, news travels very fast indeed. From California to Maine my name was equivalent to donkey dirt. Phone calls to people who were supposed to be my friends were never even returned.

Needless to say I was down for quite some time. Finally I found menial work for an ambulance-chasing firm in northern New Jersey. I worked there for a year before I could face another interview, if I could find one. I got my present job because I knew someone who knew someone, which, believe me, is the worst way to re-start a career. Anyway, I'm doing okay now, but I'll never be as good as I should have been in the first place. You don't come back from an early knockout, ever. That punch always stays with you.

Steve's story is typical of many others we could have used. There are literally hundreds of persons who have all the right credentials from the right schools who still blow it because they have unrealistic expectations about working and more self-confidence than can be fairly tested in corporate competitions. Like Steve, they not only learn the hard way but they carry that scar forever. The self-esteem never quite seems to come back.

What did Steve fail to do during his first year? To begin with, he oversold himself. His résumé claimed competencies he really didn't have, despite his education. Steve is not the only person who suffers in our society from *assumed* knowledge. Today colleges and universities turn out persons with degrees in everything from astrophysics to zoology. They title courses that later appear on transcripts in popular language (for prospective employers), and make no real effort to distinguish among quality levels of instructors and instruction. So it is not only possible, but highly probable, that two individuals graduating from the same college with exactly the same transcripts will have vastly *dissimilar* educations. Does a person with a bachelor's degree in management, at the tender age of 21, with no work experience beyond counter-clerking at Taco Bell actually know how to manage? Just because his/her transcript says he/she received passing grades in organizational behavior, consumer behavior, advanced statistics, technical writing, speech communication, and economics, should a prospective employer assume this person *knows* these subjects?

The answer, of course, is *no!* Employers have learned that most college degrees only qualify a person *to learn*; it is a license to *become* a professional, not to *be* one. Despite this understanding, those genuinely superior students who attain the highest grades and the best references are expected to know more and be able to do more than their less distinguished counterparts. Steve's career suffered from assumed excellence, a phenomenon not nearly as uncommon as you may believe. The better your résumé, the greater your burden of proof.

Steve's second error was in not adequately researching the organization to find out what his responsibilities would include during year one, or what the consequences might be if he did not perform up to standard. Had he known that two difficult law boards were in his immediate future, as well as a tough assignment, he might have been more inclined to negotiate those responsibilities, or at least the timetable for completing them. If he could have arrived at an understanding about what working for a prestigious law firm actually meant in day-to-day terms, he would have saved himself the agony of defeat. Finally, if he had known prior to accepting the position he could be terminated abruptly, and that such a termination would dramatically affect his chances to seek employment elsewhere, he might have thought twice before accepting the position.

He accurately pinpoints his third error—not being able to say "no." This is one of the absolutely essential skills of making it in any organization because you cannot be all things to all persons, nor should you try to be. To establish challenging but fair goals for oneself is the best way to begin achieving them; to establish unreachable, impossible goals for yourself is to court defeat, despair, and unemployment. While it is true the law firm might not have offered Steve the job if he squirmed over his assigned duties, it is also true if he had foreseen the consequences of his ill-fated efforts he would have perhaps tried to find meaningful work elsewhere.

Steve's fourth error was perhaps more damaging. In any organization, you need to cultivate friendly, productive working relationships with older, more experienced employees. You need a mentor. This does not mean you should become a sociopath nor a brown-nose. It does mean you need to have at least one person to go talk to when things get rough. If Steve had developed a friendly, working relationship with an older partner, he might have been able to avert disaster. Instead, he drank the wine of imagined superstardom alone, and fell from grace with his superiors. Unfortunately, those who believe they can do no wrong often fear no evil until the evil has already ruined them.

PROFILE: The following case is based on counseling interviews with Rebecca. It chronicles a broken life and does not make pleasant reading. We include it because we believe, based on our experiences in organizations, Rebecca's story, and others like it, occurs more frequently than most women's magazines care to admit.

Rebecca W. grew up in a middle-class suburb of Atlanta. She was a very attractive, talented young woman who went from captain of her cheerleading squad in high school to captain of her college debating team as if she was simply walking from one room into another. She graduated with highest honors from The University of Georgia with a degree in English Literature, and then completed a master's degree in American Literature from Vanderbilt before accepting an instructorship at Tulane University. After spending three years in New Orleans she resigned from the faculty and went back to school, this time to gain a M.B.A. from Stanford. Her career change was decided by her dissatisfaction with the salary paid to college instructors and her belief that she could do equally well in business. At 28 she entered the world of corporate business for the first time, as an analyst for a major consulting/ training corporation. Her starting salary was three times higher than her yearly earnings as a college instructor, and she was hungry to succeed. Here is her account of what happened.

Rebecca.

I guess I knew what I was doing, or at least it seemed so at the time. At ——————— I was the woman hired because they needed a woman and because the woman they needed also had to be physically attractive and experienced in educational training. Although I took my work seriously and did well at it, I was always careful to wear the latest fashions, just like in *Vogue*. I thought it was part of my job description, in a way. I mean, you know when you are the only female in the room that there is a reason for it and goals you can accomplish with it.

I started my career by playing hard to get, but soon ended up sleeping with my boss. Not a very bright thing to do, I'll admit. But I was encouraged to do so by him, and there didn't seem to be any formal sanctions against it at ———————. Also, I guess I was influenced by the feminist literature to believe that a woman had certain natural assets that could be used to advance her career, if she was careful and resourceful. In the back of my mind, I also had the old vision of a handsome prince carrying me off into the sunset. John was handsome, and he was doing very well with the company. He also was married, although he claimed he and his wife had an "open marriage." So much for the politics of simple persuasion at the motel door.

Anyway it wasn't that bad. I was a good analyst and he knew it. He helped me through my first promotion and helped me again with a major project that resulted in my second promotion that same year. But I got tired of him. I told him to go home to his wife, that it had been fun but I had to run, and that the relationship as we had known it was over. You should never say those words to your boss, believe me. He went nuts. Oh, he was always very nice to my face, but lord only knows what he told the others. Anyway, I began getting the most obvious invitations to intimacy soon after John and I broke up. I turned them all down. You see, I honestly thought I could just stop sleeping my way to the top because my performance record as an analyst was so good.

But it isn't that easy to stop being easy as that country singer puts it, which I never was but that was the general impression. It affected the quality of my work, and it affected how I felt about myself. Was I really the manipulative trollop that everyone I worked with took me for? I couldn't sleep so I took pills, which left me ragged around the edges in the mornings. Cocaine made the days easier to cope with, although snorting $100 a day worth of nose candy did put a definite strain on my income. And those damned lurid sexual invitations just kept on coming. Would I like to spend the weekend in San Francisco? Would I like to share a room at the conference in Chicago? Would I like to go for a ride in this or that sports car? And so on. The problem got worse when I started accepting those offers just to ease my pain.

I contracted herpes. I'm sure you've read about it in the magazines, and believe me genital herpes is awful and forever. Unfortunately, I also contracted facial herpes, which makes my big, beautiful face look like the work of Satan for a week at a time. I was asked to put in my resignation due to the "deteriorating effects" of my disease. So I did. I believed then that I could start fresh someplace else.

I changed jobs a good bit over the next three years. No matter where I went my reputation wasn't far behind. Although I quit doing drugs and went into transcendental meditation, I didn't really feel any better. Of course my old friend Mr. Herpes erupted every now and then to remind me of all that I desperately wanted to forget. To end it all in one swift stroke seemed to be the only way out, but at committing suicide I am a miserable failure. The shrinks here say that I really don't want to die, but they don't have to go through life being me. I'm in therapy because I can't do anything else. My future is secure so long as I remain in treatment because my last employer's health insurance is footing the bill. But if I go back out there into the real world, I'm afraid that it will just all happen again, and again, and. . . .

Rebecca's story is tragic because it didn't have to happen that way. While television movies, daytime dramas, and women's magazines often encourage women to go from bedroom to boardroom, to attract attention to their natural assets rather than their acquired ones, their depiction of corporate reality is both demeaning and unrealistic. In the real world, there are no "casual affairs" between "consenting adults." Every affair is important to both the participants and the whispering crowd back at the office. Although sexual affairs usually begin with joined organs, they usually develop into shared situations involving hearts, minds, and egos. Our survey of over 4000 individuals strongly suggests that the old double standard is still in vogue—men are more likely to be forgiven their transgressions despite the fact that most corporations have strict policies against such behavior.[4] Women fare far less well in sexual politics because their violations tend to be interpreted as flaws in their *characters* (which can be easily exploited), rather than as simply trying to have a good time.

Sleeping your way to the top is an ineffective strategy despite our so-called liberal attitudes and general permissiveness. This does not mean that you won't be asked for sexual favors; it means that you should not, under any conditions, give in to those requests. One truth from equity research should serve as a practical guide to every potentially consenting adult: The more often you bestow a reward, the less valuable it becomes.[5] Or, as the novelist Barry Hannah puts it, "anything done thrice becomes boring."

Rebecca's story also points out the often neglected, but vitally important element of good health for any successful person. She couldn't sleep so she relied on *pills*. How many times have you heard accounts of similar drug abuses by otherwise sensible, intelligent human beings? If you can't sleep, get more rigorous exercise or learn to get by on less sleep. Sleeping pills are a decadent,

[4]See G.M. Phillips and H.L. Goodall, Jr., *Loving and Living* (Englewood Cliffs, N.J.: Prentice-Hall/Spectrum Books, 1983).

[5]See E. Walster, G.W. Walster, and E. Bersheid, *Equity Theory & Research* (Boston: Allyn & Bacon, 1978).

capitalistic indulgence that promote suffering in the name of relief! (Remember, we are not physicians but we do believe in a practical approach to good health.) Cocaine may be a charming way to start the day, but it is also a deadly way to end a promising career. John DeLorean's ordeal as an accused drug dealer should point out that no matter who or what you are, if your name is linked to drugs you are finished as well as jailed. And, as in the tragic case of comedian John Belushi, you may be dead as well.

Good health is a process, not a goal. Good health requires daily care, not occasional fanaticism. Many corporations recognize the value of health by offering their employees stress reduction courses, executive fitness diet and exercise programs, and pay their medical benefits as well. However, the attainment of good health is ultimately the responsibility of the individual person, not the organization. As Rebecca's story demonstrates, the choices, as well as the consequences of those choices, are ultimately *yours* to endure.

Now that you have read how some individuals have made it and others have chosen not to, you should be ready to consider some of the practical advisories that can guide you through year one with nary a nick or a scratch (well, "nary" is the appropriate qualifier for that claim . . .). In the remaining pages of this chapter, we provide our guide to success during the first year of life in any organization.

LOCATING COMMUNICATION CHANNELS AND NETWORKS

Talk is the substance of any organization. Talk allows you to meet and greet people, to ask for and to carry out instructions, to exchange information and persuasion, and to have some fun on the job. Therefore, whom you talk to and what you talk about will, to a large extent, determine how you spend your day and how you plan for your future.

This section of the chapter explores the possibilities for locating and using communication channels and networks to further your understanding of the organization, to adapt to changes, and to control your opportunities for career advancement. First, what is a communication channel? A communication channel is defined as how talk gets to someone else, which includes its travel through air waves and light particles as well as any interferences that may distort or disrupt the message *en route*. If this sounds like a technical definition it is; however, as you will see it is important to have a technical understanding of communication channels so you can spot danger and avoid some of the tragedies of talk that may harm you.

For example, you may labor under the false assumption that when you, as a subordinate in your organization, approach your boss with the purpose of gaining information, she or he will simply listen and then politely respond to you. Untrue. Research *strongly* indicates most bosses, most of the time, listen *least* when a subordinate initiates talk.[6] Furthermore, researchers have also discovered bosses believe they communicate more often and more effectively with subordinates than they actually do and subordinates ought to regard what the boss says as important.[7] These findings show it is dangerous to assume an "open channel" for communication exists. Bosses are hard to reach and rarely listen unless the information gets to them through the appropriate channels.[8]

No channel for communication is completely "open." Your task is to find effective ways to reach the brass. Here are some basic rules to keep in mind:

—Communication between superiors and subordinates is characterized by a concern for *the accomplishment* of tasks. If you approach a superior with personal, non-task related talk, your superior may see *your* message in relation to your ability to carry out assigned duties.[9]

---

[6] See H.L. Goodall, Jr., *op. cit.*; see also A. Tennebaum, *Dyadic Communication in Industry* (Ph.D. Dissertation, The University of California, 1970), and E.E. Lawler, *et al.*, "Managers Attitudes Toward Interaction Episodes," *Journal of Applied Psychology*, 52 (1968), 432–439.

[7] See R.A. Webber, "Perceptions of Interactions Between Superiors and Subordinates," *Human Relations*, 23 (1970), 235–248.

[8] F.M. Jablin, *op. cit.*, pp. 1208–1209.

[9] See J.E. Baird, Jr., *An Analytical Field Study of Open Communication as Perceived by Supervisors, Subordinates, and Peers.* (Ph.D. Dissertation, Purdue University, 1973), and K.H. Roberts and C.A. O'Reilly, "Failures in Upward Communication: Three Possible Culprits," *Academy of Management Journal*, 17 (1974), 205–217.

If too many personal concerns characterize your talk your superior may decide you are unable to perform competently, or you are seeking a friendship or sexual relationship with him or her.

—Successful communication between superiors and subordinates is characterized by a mutual sense of exchange and reciprocity. However, many subordinates view their superiors as persons to speak at rather than to listen to, and hence create inequity. This problem is complicated further by subordinates' interest in developing relationships with influential individuals within the organization. Very often subordinates do not recognize they must offer something of value in return for the support of an influential person.

—Superiors tend to overestimate the knowledge and understanding possessed by subordinates.[10] Hence, when a subordinate fails to meet the superior's expectations, the superior is likely to blame the subordinate for incompetence rather than try to discuss how the problems actually occurred (remember Steve's case?).

—There does not appear to be "influence-free" communication in an organization. Despite recent trends to minimize the impact of hierarchies on task performance, or to sensitize persons to fairness between women and men at work, mishandling communication with your superior or your co-worker of the opposite sex will lead to disharmony and quite possibly disrespect. In other words, you can't "just talk" to someone, anyone, in an organizational context without the understanding that whatever you say can and probably will be used against you (remember Rebecca's case?).[11]

The point of this discussion is to encourage you to see talk with others as *performances* rather than intermissions in the everyday drama of work. Remember, your communication is the substance of your organizational relationships. Your communication also creates the interpersonal realities that govern the success or failure of those relationships. During your first year of work, you need to think of your communication channels with others as extended opportunities to contribute to the "first" impression you make on these individuals.

Now let's consider the importance of communication networks. There are three types of communication networks that you

[10]G.S. Odiorne, "An Application of the Communication Audit," *Personnel Psychology*, 7 (1954), 235–243.

[11]This may be particularly true for women, even with other women, see M. A. Fitzpatrick, "Think Like a Man, Talk Like a Lady," in J.J. Pilotta (Ed.), *Women in Organizations* (Prospect Heights, Ill.: Waveland Press, 1983).

need to know about. *Formal* networks include relationships with superiors, co-workers, and subordinates as described by the organizational chart. *Informal* networks include your associations with friends and acquaintances who provide you with information, rumors, gossip, and informal ways of accomplishing tasks. *Integrated* networks include a fusion of formal and informal networks that control professional and social effectiveness.

During your first year, you should develop these relationships carefully. Simply pouring your heart out to someone you work with, without considering who this person may pass the information to, is dangerous. Not only is this a perfect way to begin rumors and gossip about you, it is also a way to prevent access to important, influential persons who may have "heard about you" through their informal network. Think about it this way: What do persons talk most about during work and after hours? The answer is "other people at work" and their problems. Because you want to influence others' perceptions of you and your competencies, you must control what others say about you. This does *not* mean you should avoid conversations with others; it means you should remember information you provide may find its way elsewhere. During the first year, you must control what others say about your professional competencies and personality.

A second issue is *which networks to associate with*. You need formal and informal connections. Persons who fair poorly during their first year tend to tip the balance toward informal, friendship-based interactions at the expense of purposeful communication with their superiors, subordinates, and co-workers. It is also wise to remember that "there are networks, and then there are *networks*." Virtually any organization is comprised of valuable and less valuable employees, persons who accomplish a great deal and persons whose accomplishments are easily forgotten. If you choose to interact with persons who have a reputation for doing a good job, then the chances are you may be seen as similarly important. If you choose to associate with losers, your accomplishments will mean less to those whose job it is to locate and reward talent. It *is* more difficult to cultivate relationships with successful individuals than with losers. One reason successful persons succeed is they *limit* their relationships with others.

Sex is a third issue in communication networks. At the height of the Women's Movement, women were encouraged to develop same-sex networks to protect and to promote their common interests. One result was alienation from the opposite sex, or at least a failure to integrate formal and informal channels. However, the good of working relations between the sexes is complicated by sexual images and urgencies.[12] We may be evolving toward "synergy" between the sexes, but clearly some of us are evolving more rapidly than others. Some men still view women as objects of desire regardless of their professional competencies or marital relationships, and some women still view their organs as appropriate mechanisms for advancement.

We believe you must develop formal, informal, and integrated networks during your first year on the job. These networks are valuable because they provide you with quicker, sometimes more detailed, or more accurate information with which to do your job. The salient point to remember is to use these networks to enhance your job performance rather than to detract from it. You will be judged constantly not only by what you know, but also by the quality of your connections within the organization. Nobody who ever worked her or his way to the top ever did so alone.

LEARNING YOUR JOB FROM THE INSIDE OUT AND THE OUTSIDE IN

As far as any organization is concerned, your basic identity is your job discription. Most organizations expect you to know how to perform your duties because of your education and work experience. For most of us, entry into an organization is marked by a brief (most often *too brief*) "orientation" followed by the assignment of a particular task. The orientation usually includes how to gain access to the building, where the restrooms are located, introduction to key personnel, and you are finally asked if you have any questions. That's it. From this point on you are more or less on your own,

---

[12]See G.M. Phillips and J.T. Wood, *Communication and Human Relationships* (New York: Macmillan, 1983).

despite claims made to the contrary by your "orienter," who may tell you "to come by my office if you have any problems."

You will have problems. For example, you may be told what to do, but you may not be told the standard operating procedures for accomplishing it. You may be given a deadline, but you may not be informed about how to request a change in the deadline should a need arise. You may be assigned technical and human resources to help you complete your assignment, but not be told how the machines work or how the support personnel typically function. You may be told that you are to report to someone only to find out that someone doesn't know you from Adam. *Help!!!*

Learning to do your job is far more complicated than most organizations lead you to believe it will be. The usual scenario is you are given a destination to reach, and you are somehow supposed to find your way to it. Once the goal for your work has been articulated you ought to be able to accomplish it, right?

Wrong. There is a substantive difference between knowing *what* you are supposed to accomplish and *how* it can or should be done. This is what we mean when we say you need to "learn your job from the inside out and the outside in." Simply put, you need to contact these persons with whom you will work and to whom you will report and discover what they know and what they expect from you. Here is what you need to find out:

—About those with whom you will work, or whom you are supposed to direct:
  • What their names are; how long they have been with the organization; what their specific job duties are; what has already been accomplished pertaining to those assigned duties; and the major problems that you should know about.
—About those persons to whom you must report:
  • What their names are; how long they have been with the organization; what their specific job duties are; what has already been accomplished on this task; what remains to be accomplished; what problems exist with the task; how you are supposed to reach them in case new problems arise; what timetable or formal schedule has been developed for this task; who you can talk to about the project if they are not available; and what procedure for reporting progress on the task they prefer you to use.

This information may shape specific goals for your communication with superiors, co-workers, and subordinates. It can help you create a positive impression, one that leads others to believe you are a task-oriented individual, a worthy competitor. Besides, the answers you get to these questions will be important sources of information about how to demonstrate your competencies and to whom they must be demonstrated. Learning your job from "the inside out" will help you *communicate purposefully* with those persons who evaluate your accomplishments.

Now let's examine how you can learn your job from "the outside in."

Most persons suffer from "task blindness." This means that we tend to view our task as the *only* one going on at the time. Hence, we ignore communication directed at us from others about *their* work that could alert us to the general functioning of the organization. Moreover, by signalling to others that we are less interested in the status of their project than we are in touting our own, we may inadvertently provide negative impressions about ourselves to those who maintain channels and networks of communication elsewhere in the organization. You need to learn how others *outside of* your own task group regard the work you are doing. Listen to how one employee of a large computer software company learned the importance of finding out about her job from "the outside in":

Alice.

I was hired to do training manuals for a large project. I was told that my task "had priority" with the technical support personnel, which included a group of word processing operators and technical writers. I assumed this meant that I could get these folks to do work on my project anytime. I had a friend who worked in the technical writing department who told me, one day at lunch, that her staff was burdened with work from "priority" deadlines. But it was the kind of talk you tend to ignore because you assume she was just complaining. The next day I tried to get our manuals printed only to find out that *seventeen different projects* maintained "priority status."

Hence, my project was not completed on time. If I had only listened more carefully during that lunchtime conversation. . . .

A second issue involves the history of the organization. Through formal and informal communication, you can learn how the organization has grown and what changes have taken place. This may be the most important history lesson in your life. Although most of us unwittingly act as if history begins with our own birth and develops right along with us, there is much to be gained in learning how your organization evolved. You may find persons within the company who used to do your job, and who can tell you why certain procedures were implemented, how to get around needless red tape, or how to approach your current boss. Finding your way around any organization during the first year should include a trip through corporate history via the words of persons who contributed to it.

Finally, it is important to learn what others consider to be appropriate standards for your work. Although you may work directly under a particular supervisor or manager, his or her standards may not be the *company's* standards. If this is the case, you may need to keep more detailed records of your activities—after all, your present boss may be fired and you would have to inform your new superior about the status of current work. If your ex-boss maintained lower standards than your new boss prefers, you may find yourself in trouble without having actually done anything wrong. Another possibility might be that *you* suddenly find yourself promoted to your old boss's position, and unfortunately find you don't have all the necessary documentation you need. However, if *you* have kept detailed, accurate records of your work it will be easier to establish new standards for your subordinates based on what you have learned from others in the organization.

Learning how to perform your job takes time and effort. You should learn how to ask questions designed to gain access to public and private information about your job, how your job fits into the organization, and the standards used to evaluate job performance. To answer these important questions requires talking to others without appearing to waste their time or infringe on their job performance. It will also mean developing the skill of being friendly without committing yourself to any friendships or intimacies. Sound confusing? Continue reading, the next section of this chapter investigates making friends, being friendly, and making enemies on the job.

MAKING FRIENDS, BEING FRIENDLY, AND MAKING ENEMIES DURING YEAR ONE, OR, HOW TO GET THEM TO KNOW YOU WITHOUT KNOWING YOU TOO WELL . . .

Nobody likes to be alone in the company of others. When you begin a new job, one of the primary considerations is usually "will I get along with the people who work there?" As you become acculturated at work, one of your day-to-day concerns is "how am I seen and judged by these people?" You may want to make a good first impression, but after the first few days you become attuned to keeping your professional image sharp, making and keeping communication networks, and engaging in routine pleasantries that characterize good manners in any organization.

Most of us are reared with the myth of friendship. We expect to make many friends, engage in activities with other people, go to and from work with others who share our interests and concerns, and be friendly to the human race, especially to old folks, young children, and warm, helpless puppies. Through the 12 years of socialization processing that passes for basic education in this country, we are encouraged implicitly and explicitly to acquire the skills of friend-making, including polite conversation, reciprocity of exchange, and friendly argument (however, our schools seldom provide training in these necessary skills!!). During these periods of learning we develop "personalities," usually based on the responses we have received to our attempts at communication and friendship/intimacy with others. But we also develop a deeply rooted belief in the myths of friendship, such as:

—You should be friends with everyone, particularly those persons who most need a friend.

—You should develop as many friends as possible because the more friends you have the less likely you will be lonely and the more likely you will become popular and successful.

—You should be totally honest with your friends.

—You should be willing to disclose intimate information to your friends because a friend will never betray you.

—There are important differences between friends and lovers. Therefore, you shouldn't try to escalate a friendship into a romance or intimate relationship.

—You shouldn't admit having enemies.

Each of these myths damages your ability to actually make and keep friends. For example, the myth that you "should be friends with everyone, particularly those who need a friend" denies you the opportunity to select your friends carefully or to avoid sociopathic individuals who will abuse your friendship as an addict abuses drugs. The myth "you should develop as many friends as possible . . ." encourages you to do the impossible; friendship requires time and mutual effort, and when you are trying to advance a career you have little of either. To become friends is to commit yourself to regular interaction and caring, something most successful persons limit rather than encourage. The third and fourth myths are closely related. Should you be "totally honest . . . and be willing to disclose private information" to your friends? We don't think so, at least based on the 4000 persons we sampled for our study of friendship. Those persons in our sample who reported having meaningful friendships of the nondestructive variety were careful what they disclosed and occasionally sacrificed total honesty for an unwillingness to intentionally hurt their friends. The fifth myth concerning the supposed wrongness of pursuing romance with a friend is a mixed blessing. On the one hand it is true—you should remember that there are important differences between friends and lovers and you should act accordingly. On the other hand, it is often wiser to develop a close friendship with someone before loving them than to simply base love on physical attraction or sexual gratification. Finally, the sixth myth says you should have no enemies. Yet people do have enemies, and in an organizational setting you may be known by the quality of your enemies.

What Is an Enemy?

In the olden days, persons used to believe in demons and evil spirits and witches—the "enemies" of good and prosperous living, the "slithy toves" to be avoided. The great Talmudic traditions say these evil spirits and demons can be found in the character of negative individuals, and Christian traditions validate this assumption by revealing how Satan can take human forms. From the equally great Eastern mystic religions we can locate the presence of evil in persons who do not balance the yin and yang of their lives, who triumph over their friends and relatives through acts of deceit, cunning, lying, and cheating. From all the world's great religions we find the common shape of evil as manifested in bad persons, those sinister individuals who worship Faust's image at the expense of their own soul, equity with others, and the peace of the world.

Modern science challenges the legitimacy of religious beliefs on a number of levels, but on the question of evil beings there is an odd consensus between believers and researchers. Behavioral scientists and criminologists agree that some persons are just plain "bad," either through genetic or environmental influences. These persons may commit hideous crimes against humanity or they may live next door, quietly plotting against you and yours. Not all the bad people are safely under prison security nor do they always get caught in the act of committing crimes. The point here is negative individuals, whether they have sold their souls to Satan or merely suffer from genetic miscoding, do exist and are perfectly willing to do you harm should your innocent path suddenly cross theirs.

An enemy is someone who has the potential and desire to do you harm. An enemy is a bad person, from your point of view. However, there are enemies, and then there are *enemies*. For instance, you may have a friend who is technically and temporarily your "enemy" simply because you both are forced to compete for the same rewards—a promotion, a raise, a mortgage on a house, or a professional opportunity. While you compete you may both see each other a little differently, maintaining the grace of friendship in public and conjuring up demons in private. This form of enemyship is common and relatively harmless because the evil acts are confined to mental scenarios in which you do battle.

A second form of enemyship raises the potential to commit evil acts to actual acts of war. This is the enemy who will go out of his or her way to do you harm, and who will stir up the emotions of others against you through bearing false witness, lying, stretching the truth, or being deceitful. This form of enemy relies on the crowd to do his or her bidding, and who actively attempts to shape the emotions of the crowd against you. In an office setting, this is the enemy who uses the network to spread rumors and gossip about others, and to call into being the will of the group against those individuals who he or she wants to destroy. Beware of the gossip monger, for you never know when she or he will turn his or her nasty tongue against *you*. The cause for harmdoing may be your looks, your good name, your promise for promotion, your achievements, or simply your existence on the planet Earth.

A third form of enemyship is the demonic, depraved, dehumanized devil whose intent to do harm becomes an intent to end your life, either by getting you fired without references or by actually murdering you. We usually associate this ultimate form of evil with mindless killers who shoot at strangers from rooftops or who munch the bones of their in-laws and hide the remains in a freezer or bury them in a frontlawn—the kind of act reported in cheap journalistic newspapers or on the comparatively tame nightly news. We seldom associate this form of deviltry with the politics of an office or a profession, and hence increase our chances to become victims by negating our awareness that these acts of evil are occasionally committed in organizations like ours, against persons like us. We believe in detective and espionage fiction *á la* John Le Carre, Agatha Christie, or John MacDonald, but we cling to the hope that "those things just don't happen in real life." We read daily newspapers or weekly magazines and are entertained by reports of violence and wrongdoing in corporate America, and yet refuse to admit that there are persons lurking near the water cooler who willfully plot our destruction. Such are the simple paradoxes of our minds, paradoxes that become frightfully real when we find out who-said-what-to-whom-with-what-effect, or, in the case of some unfortunate women, what the real intent is of that nice man who works down the hall when he waits by the door after hours.

You need to develop a sense of skepticism about the persons you work with and for. You need to accept that persons, including yourself, are capable of doing both good and evil in this world, and very often the difference between "good" and "evil" is a matter of perspective. You need to watch out for the other guy and gal because you never know why he or she might be sneaking up to or sneaking away from you.

This does not mean you should become a paranoid, or that you should carry a weapon at all times. It means you should admit that despite your inherent goodness and charm someone else may dislike you and wish you harm. It means you should avoid disclosing personal information, such as intimate details of your love life and personal feelings about your boss or secretary, to anyone with whom you work and compete for rewards. It means you should try not to arm your enemies by providing them with verbal ammunition or information ripe for gossip. And it means you should monitor the communication of others at all times, listening carefully for those cues that signal the potential for harmdoing.

But what can you do if you find out you have an enemy? Obviously, you do have choices to make. You can confront the person, ask them why he or she wishes you harm, and wait for the likely denial of all charges. You can admit this person is your enemy and attempt to regain equity by direct retaliation—an eye for an eye, a rumor for a rumor. Unfortunately, this tactic usually wastes time and energy at the expense of productivity and allows others to see the potential for evil in you which may alter their association with you, or at least alter the reasons for associating with you. You could privately store up your hatreds for one big public tantrum in which you denounce your enemy, but then you have to suffer more time privately than you have to carry out your public revenge and you risk being seen as a freak when you do explode. Or you could make the all-too-common mistake of saying to every Sally and Bob that comes your way: "Hey, did you hear what x said about me?" Most persons will not care what "x" said about *you* unless it directly affects them. Besides, if you hide in the crowd from an enemy, you risk appearing weaker than you need to.

Consider your enemy to be your equal. Too many persons

make their enemies into strong, alien images that become too abstract to deal with personally. Do not devalue your enemy or else you risk underestimating the damage she or he can and will do unto you. Then collect information about him or her quietly. Do not divulge the purpose of your inquiries, nor your intent to do harm. Everyone has weaknesses, skeletons in the closet, or drives which, if made public, would appear ridiculous. The reason for gathering information about your enemies is simply to learn about how they act, what they think, incidences of their personal and corporate histories, and why they might hate you. *Keep this information to yourself!* When you think you know enough about them *to make accurate predictions about their future behavior*, you are ready to act.

How you act depends on the degree of acceptable escalation of the war between you, and on the strength of your remaining desire to get even. But do not let your emotions prevent you from rationally thinking through the consequences of your revenge. Who might turn against you should your strategy ever be revealed? Is the glory of your revenge worth the potential negative costs? For most persons, most of the time, learning about enemies is enough because the more accurate your assessment of their character and behavior, the less likely they will be able to harm you. If you can find a quiet way to let them know how much you know about them, you gain the satisfaction of having the potential to do them harm but never having to use it. This is known as diplomacy, or if the stakes are high enough between you, then "mutually assured destruction." But remember, you can usually only act against an enemy *once*; after that time, your intentions and storehouse of ugly information will be public record. Most evil persons can be more easily defeated by knowledge than by direct displays of power.

Making friends and enemies is a natural part of living, loving, and working. Knowing *how* to make friends and neutralize enemies is an acquired talent, based as all active attempts to create personal and social realities are based, in the communication acts that constitute who you are and what you do. We cannot stress enough the importance of monitoring your talk with others, for the difference between a friend and an enemy may fall on the words you speak far more often than on the acts you perform.

MAXIMS FOR MAKING IT THROUGH THE FIRST YEAR

No discussion of your first year in organizations is complete without a handy-dandy list of maxims, drawn from the experiences of those giving the information. Here is ours:

1. *Manage your personal image:* There is an entirely appropriate logic to "dressing for success." Because first impressions never get a second chance to happen, and because we are a society dependent on adaptations to environment and the opinions of others, it makes good sense to dress in good taste. Usually this means choosing conservative styles, at least initially. There is a good reason why Brooks Brothers shirts have not changed styles since 1914—they are *always* tasteful and understated. There was an excellent reason for the IBM "uniform"—credibility is often attributed to persons who remind us of other persons we have judged competent or trustworthy. Managing your personal image in today's competitive marketplace is as important as learning the skills of leadership or computer programming. It is truly not only what you know how to do, but also how you look while accomplishing your tasks that gain the attention of superiors. Women, however, must guard *which* attentions they are inducing because a sensuous, smart woman sexually attired is difficult to deal with without considering her physical assets to be intentional advertisements.

2. *Staying physically fit:* Success in any organization takes time. If you burn out before you are 40, you limit your options as well as damage your health. Staying physically fit reduces fat, increases your ability to handle stress, and allows most persons to get by on far less sleep than the standard eight hours. You may also feel better. However, do not advertise your healthiness in the office because your old, overweight, sleepless, sexless boss may very well hold it against you.

3. *Finding recreation:* "All work and no play makes Jack/Jill a dull person," and it is as true today as it was in the beginning. You need to cultivate productive hobbies, sources of fun, and entertainment. These should *not* include hanging out in singles' bars looking horny and homeless, nor should they include becoming a

victim of video-games or the tube. Enrich your life, your storehouse of knowledge, and your ability to compete by finding recreation that is worthwhile. Playing tennis, squash, racquetball, or jogging seem to be acceptable sports for the rising organizational person. Bowling, golf, and beer-drinking seem less appropriate either because they cater to the tastes of the lower classes or older generations. It is probably unfair to equate golf with bowling, but these are our prejudices and you must develop your own. One of the authors believes that racquetball is a tediously middle-class sport and refuses to play, and finds arguing the point with friends to be his source of recreation.

4. *Neither a borrower nor a lender be:* One of the cultural by-products of making a decent living is the ability to buy on credit. VISA, MasterCard, and American Express all point out the advantages of "not leaving home without them," and yet each year many otherwise competent professionals get in trouble with debt. Because money problems cannot be left at home, they are sources of personal as well as professional demise. Borrow wisely. Lending money can also be a problem, particularly if the person to whom you lend it cannot afford to pay it back, or bases your friendship on it.

5. *Showing off in style:* Everyone wants to stand out in the working crowd. Some persons do it by attaining high levels of literacy, others do it by building better stereo systems than the ear can appreciate. The thing to avoid is showing off your knowledge or possessions in ways that either intimidate or devalue the tastes of others. In the next chapter, we discuss how to become a tasteful snob by cultivating your pleasures, but the point of becoming a creative snob is to enrich your own life, not to make others seem less important than they are. After all, you can be thought knowledgeable and despised for it or you can be thought knowledgeable and valued because of it—the choice is not *to be or not to be* knowledgeable; instead, the choice is how to *communicate* what you know.

This chapter addressed the importance of your first year in any organization. Remember, your career can resemble Jason's or Rebecca's—the choice ultimately is yours.

Your First Year I.Q. Enhancer

1. Colleges and universities do seem to prepare us for careers without helping us make it through the first year on a job. Name three specific differences between school and work life that ought to guide your choices of behavior.

2. Why are informal channels and networks often more effective and efficient means of gaining information than formal ones? If this is the case, then why don't organizations make more productive use of informal channels and networks? Why does it always seem to come down to that?

3. Why do you need friends at work? Don't you have any at home? Do you need to feel included because you are so afraid of being excluded, or is it because you are basically paranoid? Or is it really because unless you are surrounded by some friendly people, you will be consumed by your feelings of hostility, aggression, and hatred? Now, do *you* have any enemies? Think again. Don't you fundamentally believe most persons are pretty much like you are? Now name your enemies.

4. Why did Oscar Wilde say "If you find yourself in a situation in which the good people are rewarded and evil people are punished, then you are living in a novel." Was he just a mean person, or is this rare insight? Justify your answer based on what happened at work today.

5. If we learn from our mistakes, but our mistakes are held against us, how can we profit from what we learned by making them? Do you think this is a reason why people change jobs so frequently these days? Isn't changing your job a way of starting over without having the past held eternally against you?

chapter five

HOW TO BE A
LIKEABLE SNOB

"Our opinions become fixed at the point where we stop
thinking."

—JOSEPH RENAN

"Talk is by far the most accessible of pleasures. It costs nothing
in money, it is all profit, it completes our education, founds
and fosters our friendships, and can be enjoyed at any age and
in almost any state of health."

—ROBERT LOUIS STEVENSON

"Living well is the best revenge."

—OSCAR WILDE

AN INTRODUCTION TO THE LOGIC OF SNOBBERY

The logic of "how to succeed in business" maintains that organizations reward persons who demonstrate competency in the work
assigned to them, leadership among their peers, and social graces
in all matters public and private. We agree with the basic tenets of
this philosophy of success, but to it we add this chapter on developing the singular talent of snobbery.

Being a snob means you are able to appreciate and do things other people can't. Before we go any further, though, we need to distinguish real snobbery from the more common, less appreciable phony variety.

A great many persons are phony snobs. They read only the Sunday papers, but quote unmercifully from them as if they read all the books cited and experienced all the sensations of living in the modern world. They correct your grammar as if William Safire had been their mentor and close friend, and the *Harbrace Handbook* their guide to good living. They remove the television sets from their living rooms and claim they don't need to watch it anymore, speaking their trite little speech as a testament to their impeccable tastes and their infinite wisdom (actually, we have found that persons who make this boring claim usually sneak off to watch the tube they so despise when they think others won't notice, and they can be caught making references to shows they claim not to have seen). These are not real snobs. To be a real snob means to cultivate tastes and activities for your own personal pleasure. It is not important whether anyone else shares them, although you may appreciate others who can share similar experiences with you. Phony snobbery is a put-on; the purpose is to put-down others who do not share your manufactured sensibilities. Hence, we dedicate this chapter to those few, fortunate individuals who want to become real snobs, who want to earn the rights and privileges associated with enjoying the best life has to offer without giving up their sense of humility and compassion.

The logic of snobbery begins with an appreciation of the relationship between acquiring good information and making productive use of it. You can't be a successful snob if you don't have good information upon which to develop your appeal. By good information we mean a general understanding of history, culture, science, literature, and the arts, and carefully acquired specific information about those topics that *you* find most interesting and enjoyable. For example, you may have a college degree but this doesn't automatically mean you have developed good taste or good sense. Neither does it mean you have ever studied history (we don't mean memorized the important dates for an exam!), or reflected upon the words contained in passages drawn from great literatures (we don't mean read the crude outlines provided for persons who need them to write term papers). You may have a transcript showing passing grades in the general liberal arts and sciences curriculum, but do you *really know* enough about any of those subjects to hold a decent conversation with someone who does know enough to speak plainly about them?

From a practical perspective, how you answer the above question is critically important because it provides you with insight about what it is that you do (or do not) know. *If you cannot hold a conversation with someone who has knowledge of your topic, then you probably don't know enough about it to appreciate and enjoy it.* Here is the elegance of the relationship between possessing knowledge and being able to act upon it. Knowledge for knowledge's sake is important if you spend your life alone; knowledge for the sake of conversation and intensified pleasure is important if you want to become a successful snob.

The second supposition of successful snobbery is that being a snob doesn't give you license to put other people down for not sharing your interests. You may want to talk about the finer points of cross-over wiring strategies for stereo speaker systems, but unless your partner in the conversation can profit from your discussion, or contribute to it in a meaningful way, then you are engaging in conversational masturbation, not conversational elegance. When you involve someone else in your favorite topic, you need to recognize that your interest in it may not be shared, in fact, does not have to be shared. For if you are really a snob, you don't acquire satisfaction from eliciting boredom and feelings of stupidity from others. Instead, you acquire satisfaction from the thing itself, for the experience of knowing, being, and doing that comes from your personal understandings.

The third tenet of successful snobbery is being able to induce others *who demonstrate an interest* in your topic to become more interested in it. The likeable snob is a person who doesn't mind sharing her or his information, if the invitation to share it comes from someone else. All you need to do is bring up the subject, check to see how others respond to it, and then decide whether or not you should continue discussing it. Let the responses you receive from others be your guide.

Finally, the logic of snobbery would indeed be incomplete if we didn't state that *there are strategic advantages to be accrued from becoming a likeable snob*. In a recent survey, business executives were polled concerning the characteristics of success. The findings may surprise you. First, most of the executives surveyed said they saw a distinct trend among the managerial and professional ranks in their organizations. Those persons most likely to succeed not only were knowledgeable in their fields of expertise, they were also well-informed citizens in the classic tradition—knowledgeable in history, science, politics, the arts, and current affairs. The day of the narrow specialist may well be over!! Second, the persons most likely to succeed were *interesting persons*. Not only did they do their jobs well, they were engaging conversationalists, able to talk about matters and interests well beyond their formal training. They read books, magazines, and newspapers; they took exciting vacations; they shared their experiences with others. And finally, they were able to *communicate effectively* with almost everyone—not just their immediate peers or supervisors. These persons are rare. And that is why they are most likely to succeed—they really do stand out among the maddening crowd.

To become a likeable snob is not easy. It requires what is most difficult for most persons—to understand yourself well enough to know how to distinguish *genuine satisfaction* from the merely *satisfying*. It also requires knowing where and how to seek out general and specific information about your interests. To truly be a snob requires time, effort, and the ability to select from the available sources of knowledge those most likely to reward your investments.

As you can see, being a likeable snob is a very good thing. It helps you to meet people with whom you are compatible and with whom you can share the pleasures of conversation and experience. It develops a sense of trust among the company of fellow snobs. Furthermore, it keeps you away from pressures to conform to the mediocrities of the historical moment. Snobs are rarely trampled to death at concerts, or trapped on the edges of existential despair.

They are rarely drug addicts, and they almost never require psychiatric treatment. Best of all they are never, ever bored. That is because successful snobs can "fill each golden minute with 60 seconds worth of distance run." They can be alone without being lonely, they rarely resent the company they choose to associate with, and they are able to balance their obligations with their pleasures. Here are our recommendations, categorized according to our own snobbish interests.

BOOKS TO READ

Your introduction to productive snobbery begins with an appreciation of great books. These books are great because they contain within them the wisdom and challenges of good thinking, good writing, and useful information. Here is our primer for *Snobbery 101*:

Ancient Greeks and Romans: Everyone should have some contact with Plato and Aristotle, the two basic philosophical stances that have shaped Western civilization. Plato, forever the idealist, can best be appreciated through his depiction of the dialogues of Socrates, as found in *Symposium*, *Apology*, *Gorgias*, *Phaedrus*, and *The Republic*. Aristotle, forever the pragmatist, can best be appreciated through his summaries of issues as relevant and thought-provoking now as they were in his own age. Try his *Ethics*, *Metaphysics*, *Rhetoric*, and *Poetics* for starters, then move on to the *Prior and Posterior Analytics* for an appreciation of formal reasoning.

The Great Religious Treatises: Even if you claim no religion, you need to acquire an understanding of what you are discounting. For those reared as Christians, *The Holy Bible* is a must because too many persons talk about it without having ever turned a page of the work, and these days any consumer of Jerry Falwell's rhetoric needs to know the difference between his interpretation of the scriptures and what is actually there. For those reared as Jews, the *Talmud* and perhaps some of the *Kabala* provide ideas basic to the way of life and its mysteries which are worth investigating. For Eastern mysticism followers, there are many works available, and the best advice we can offer is to find the ones with the most credible translators.

Strategic Books: This category includes works designed to provide practical advisories on how to live your life. Everyone who plans a career in an organization should read Machiavelli's *The Prince* before calling someone else a "Machiavellian." We also recommend Von Clauswitz *On War*, the collected essays of Montaigne, and the marvelous guide to getting ahead in a bureaucracy, Castiglione's *The Book of the Courtier*.

Science, Scientific Explanations of Human Behavior, and the Nature of Human Society: No one breathing the air of the twentieth century should miss reading Charles Darwin's *The Origins of Species*, Sigmund Freud's *Lectures on Psychiatry* and *The Interpretation of Dreams*, Alfred Adler's *Individual Psychology*, or E.O. Wilson's *On Human Nature*. However, some of these works make tedious reading, and for this reason you may want to check out some reliable commentaries *before* embarrassing yourself with the originals. We recommend Calvin Hall's *Freudian Primer* for those persons interested in pursuing an understanding of Freud, and any number of recent critical books on other major influences, such as Adler and Jung. If you read *On Human Nature* and begin to believe in sociobiology, then you owe it to yourself to also read some of Wilson's critics, particularly Stephen J. Gould.

We would be crazy not to recommend other seminal influences such as the work of Karl Marx *(Das Capital)* and other sociologists (Max Weber, Emile Durkheim, or George Herbert Mead). As silly as most of contemporary sociology has gotten, these early thinkers provide astonishing power to their explanations of society. In that same spirit, the American pragmatists such as John Dewey, C.S. Pierce, and William James provide interesting introductions to thinking, reasoning, and knowing which are difficult, but worthwhile. It is hard to be a real snob without having investigated some of these works because you may discover your "great idea" is really a poor imitation of the original, and re-inventing the wheel is such a waste of time!

Self-Awareness Books: Most thinking persons are concerned about the norms of society, of the ways in which general human behavior acquires meaning in our own time. David Riesman's *The*

Lonely Crowd provides an accurate description of general social behavior in American society despite the fact that it was written during the 1950s. A more modern description with a different drum-
mer can be found in Christopher Lasch's *The Culture of Narcissism*,
the book about us during the post-Vietnam, post-flowerchild,
post-Watergate disco generation of the late 1970s. Richard Sennett's rich history of capitalism and its effects on the modern
psyche, in *The Fall of Public Man*, provides readers with incredibly
dense historical, cultural, architectural, and dramatic metaphors to
describe the evolutions of humans, environments, machines, and
modes of behavior since the 1800s. For especially well-written accounts of the influences of technology on us all, see Daniel
Boorstin's *The Republic of Technology* or Langdon Winner's *Au-
tonomous Technology*. And finally, on the writing of American history, see Frances FitzGerald's *America Revised*.

The Arts and Great Literature: The list here is so long it would
require a book of its own to present thoroughly. If you haven't
taken the time to browse in a good bookstore lately, you don't
know what you are missing. The local library also provides an
alternative to the three-martini lunch—libraries are good places to
be comfortable, acquire knowledge, and avoid the temptations of
mass media. Our recommendation is to visit a library, look around
slowly, and select some books you've always wanted to read. Go
ahead, do it. Develop your own preferences.

Improving Your Snob I.Q.

1. Who is Wally Shawn, and why don't most persons get to see his
   marvelous plays? Who was his father? Why does knowing father
   and son shed new light on both of them? Which one was once
   referred to as "that homunculus" in a famous Woody Allen movie?
2. Which literary critic believes the trope is essentially a psychic defense mechanism? Why is understanding this point of view so important to persons grappling with the epistemic foundations of
   rhetoric?
3. Give three arguments for the claim that William Shakespeare was
   actually Queen Elizabeth. Give two arguments for the claim that
   William Shakespeare was actually Christopher Marlowe. Give one
   argument for why none of the above arguments should matter to
   anyone.

PEAK EXPERIENCES FOR YOUR PERSONAL PLEASURE

Reading is not the only way to develop likeable snobbery. To be a truly successful snob you need to cultivate your sense of adventure through exotic traveling, dining, and imbibing. By broadening your knowledge of the planet, its citizens, and its fares, you gain what snobs the world over call "perspective." You may also have a good time. The following list provides our summary of places to go for the experience of them, places ripe for aspiring snobs.

1. *Williamsburg, Virginia:* Come here deep in winter for an experience that enlightens the mind and delights the eyes. The hotels are warm and gracious and the food is splendid—besides, you get something like authentic contact with American history.

2. *McCall, Idaho; Brighton, Utah; Vail, Colorado:* If skiing and scenery is what you find most appealing about planning a vacation, then these three spots will satisfy and inspire you. Vail may be a bit too well-known, but in summer or winter it provides an atmosphere in which sport, scenery, and general hedonism abound.

3. *New York, New York:* It is easy to wave off the Big Apple, but dollar for dollar it offers the greatest recreation in the world, and with good hotels offering special weekend rates, it is nowhere as expensive as you might think. There are great eating places, and you can queue up to buy half-price Broadway show tickets. There isn't anything you could wish for that you couldn't find somewhere in this great city.

4. *Canada, period:* The American dollar goes a long way in Canada. Toronto is a bastion of civilization and culture, Montreal is truly cosmopolitan, as is Winnipeg, Calgary has the old pioneer spirit (especially at Rodeo time—the only and nearest competition being Cheyenne, Wyoming's Frontier Days during the last week in July), and the scenery at Banff and Lake Louise can't be beat. For super-culture lovers try Niagara-on-the-Lake (not the falls) for the Shaw theatre festival or try the Stratford Shakespeare Festival.

5. *New England, in Autumn:* New England inns are generally very good places to rest and relax—some of them come with fireplaces in the bedroom and breakfast in bed, others just have the

fireplaces and all that they suggest. Do New England in the autumn, when the air is crisp, the leaves are colored, and the fireplaces so very hot indeed.

6. *Nashville, Tennessee:* For contact with what at least one of the authors calls "real Americans" try The Grand Old Opry and its counterpart Opryland. Nashville is exactly like you want it to be—a redneckish town with great music in small bars as well as a civilized city with all the modern conveniences.

7. *Chapel Hill, North Carolina:* You may have seen bumperstickers with the legend: "I'd rather be in Chapel Hill." Go there and you will want one too. Chapel Hill is the place where The University of North Carolina is located, the nation's oldest state university and unquestionably one of the finest academic institutions in the world. Their library is a scholar's delight, but the real reason for visiting is that this is what a college campus *ought* to look like and feel like, and besides, you meet the nicest people there. Many good restaurants, curiosity shops, and opportunities for pleasurable communication.

8. *A train ride, almost anywhere:* Book a Pullman roomette and enjoy the countryside, wherever it is! Then venture down to the dining car and order a memorable meal. On most trains, (but particularly the Union Pacific) they still know how to treat you right. Get into a friendly game of cards in the bar, smoke a good cigar, and get into the spirit of training. Once you enjoy a train ride, you always come back for more.

9. *The island of Antiqua:* You have to either fly or sail in to this astonishing place, but is certainly worth the effort. Antiqua is virtually untouched, unspoiled splendor with friendly folks, 365 white sand, baby blue sea beaches (one for each day of the year), incredible seafood (but you must enjoy some barbequed lobster on the beach!), and recreation opportunities (from golf to tennis to horseback riding). Of all the islands, this is the one to go to.

10. *Europe, in the old style:* You hear people tell you that you can go to Europe for very little money. This is true, but you won't enjoy it nearly as much as you will if you can spend a few thousand dollars doing Europe right. Why go there if you can't stay in the best hotels, dine on some of the world's finest food, enjoy the

pleasures of sight-seeing, touring, and so on? Backpacking is okay until you are about 21, after that it is simply tacky. Do it right the first time, and then come back again, doing Europe *your* way. We suggest beginning in Amsterdam and then going South to Rome, working your way back up through Switzerland, turning left almost anywhere and enjoying France, and then decide whether or not you want to (a) go to England, (b) go to Spain, or (c) go to Greece on a very slow boat.

11. *Gulf Shores, Alabama:* Just east of Mobile are some of the finest beaches in the world, complete with at least one Grand Hotel. Also, if you want to drive a little you can enjoy the historic ports of Mobile and New Orleans. Forget Florida unless you have relatives there who will put you up for free, or kids to take to Disney World. Instead book passage to Gulf Shores and really enjoy yourself.

If you can't afford the time to really get away, then we suggest exploring the nearest large city in your region. Most large cities have gracious hotels, good food, and intriguing neighborhoods. And remember, true snobbery begins at home.

ON ENTERTAINMENT AND GOOD FOOD

Entertainment is an important component of snobbery, provided you know what you like. One of our great presidents introduced the statement "I don't know anything about art, but I know what I like." If you know what you like, your snobbery can be successful. It will help you decide what to do with your spare time and it will guarantee some genuine contact with other people who know what they like.

1. *Theater:* Americans are fortunate because we have a great deal of theater to choose from. Broadway theater is still the best in the world if you can afford it. Shows that have "made it" through the years are available to everyone through half price "two fers" that you purchase in Times Square. Regional theater is improving, probably because there are more talented actors and actresses, as well as playwrights, than the big Apple can even accommodate.

Communities like Louisville, Hartford, Los Angeles, Cleveland, Minneapolis, and others are distinguished for their unique professional theaters, and many local universities and colleges sponsor good productions. Keep posted on the reviews and avoid seeing new shows (unless you are in New York) by unknown writers until they have run at least three months.

2. *Movies:* Movies are good bets, almost always. There are so many different movies you need to keep posted on the reviews or else you may end up watching some horrible violent bloody thing instead of the nice romance you were hoping for. TV shows such as "Sneak Previews" or "Entertainment Tonight" also offer quality film reviews.

3. *Ballet, Symphony, & Opera:* If your tastes tend toward these learned pasttimes, there are usually opportunities to enjoy them in most metropolitan areas. If you are serious about them, you should join a fund-raising group and genuinely support them. Furthermore, many of the New York-based companies tour each year, and virtually every major university sponsors series devoted to each of these entertainment options.

4. *Music:* There is enough music around to suit every conceivable taste from classical to new wave. Most persons say they enjoy "their" music, which usually translates to the music they grew up with, but you should really try a variety of styles before deciding on just one. Country music has come a long way since the early days of the Grand Ol' Opry, and rock and roll has come an equally long way since Elvis. Classical music has been enhanced by recent innovations in the recording industry, and if you haven't heard Beethoven on a direct disc recording, you haven't heard Beethoven.

5. *Television:* TV is not as bad as some of its critics make it seem. With cable and satellite channels, everyone can be satisfied. Television is a good, private source of entertainment, but it tends to limit conversation in families and supply a variety of dangerous myths about life, in general. Selective viewing is the sensible answer.

6. *Radio:* There are some special programs on radio that enlarge their publics beyond the Top 40 crowd. Talk show addicts can choose from a variety of formats in virtually every locale, and Na-

tional Public Radio provides first rate shows such as "Prarie Home Companion," Jean Shepherd's nostalgia, and the impeccable "All Things Considered." You can also find British humor, ethnic music, and every other conceivable style of music which, with the proper stereo equipment, can surround you with the sounds you love to live in.

7. *Sports:* Ours is a nation of avid sports fans and athletes. The fans usually prefer the endless varieties of sport provided by television, or an occasional night out at the arena or stadium. The athletes prefer to participate in everything from rag football in autumn to middle-aged basketball on the weekends to the company-sponsored softball league. Sports are for everybody, as the recent athleticism has poignantly pointed out. Try squash or racquetball, tennis or golf, jogging or slimnastics, skiing or skating, and so on. But do find a sport—only the dullest dullards don't have one.

8. *Museums, Zoos, and Aquariums:* Major ones of any of these are always good entertainment values. The Metropolitan Museum of Art and the Museum of Natural History in New York, the Smithsonian in Washington, the Museum of Science and Industry in Chicago, or Huntsville, Alabama's Space & Rocket Museum can provide days of educational entertainment for a few bucks. Be sure to wear comfortable shoes and take frequent breaks, or else you will inevitably suffer from information overload. Zoos and aquariums are more fun than you remembered them to have been. If you haven't visited one lately, spend an afternoon there and then tell all your friends about the experience.

9. *Conversation:* Don't forget that one of the oldest forms of human entertainment is good talk. Having friends over for a polite evening should be a cause for conversation, and sitting around with your best friend chewing the fat is one of the rarest pleasures on the planet.

Now we will appeal to one of the baser instincts—the love of good food. You can always get something to eat, but that's eating, not *dining*. If you want a good meal you should be willing to spend some time investigating options, and of course, you must be willing to pay for it. Good food hardly ever comes cheap, and although real snobs know how to get the most for their money, they are also willing to spend some extra bucks to get exactly what they like. Here is our guide to snobbish dining.

   1. *Select the restaurant carefully:* There are as many styles and varieties of preparing food as there are countries in the world and regions within those countries. But to get precisely what you want requires that you know something about cooking as well as dining out. Read James Beard's *Theory and Practice of Good Cooking*, Jacques Peppin's *Everyday Cooking*, or Craig Clayborne's *New York Times Cookbook*, try some of the recipes yourself, and *then* you may begin to appreciate what the term "good food" really means. Fools rush out to expensive restaurants and expect a noetic experience from dining out; snobs know what the best prepared food is supposed to include and taste like, and the ability to make these fine distinctions improves the pleasures of dining. When you know what you like, *then* choose a restaurant specializing in that style of cooking. But don't be a narrow-palatted snob—seek out new experiences in dining and expand your understanding and appreciation of good food.
   2. *Check the standard ratings for restaurants:* The *Mobile Travel Guide*, *Gourmet*, *Holiday*, and *Food and Wine* are some of the better rating sources for restaurants. Most newspapers also publish ratings and/or reviews of local eating establishiments. Recommendations from friends who have acquired the ability to distinguish good cooking from "they give you a whole lot of food" are welcomed.
   3. *Always make a reservation:* Enough said.
   4. *Keep a record of fine dining experiences:* Ditto.

If you find yourself in a new town and don't know where to get a decent meal, there are ways to spot a good restaurant. Asking whether or not the food is prepared on the premises doesn't guarantee quality—these days even very good restaurants make use of prepackaged food and it will be "prepared" on the premises. There is nothing wrong with prepackaging except that substitutions are usually not possible. When you see a miniscule *á la carte* section of the menu with a thorough selection of three-course meals you can bet the restaurant buys prepackaged food, defrosts it, heats it, and serves it to you. You could think of it as a fancy TV dinner. . . .

To be sure the restaurant you are entering is a good place:

1. Look for a restaurant associated with name of a chef and ask whether or not the chef is on the premises.
2. Look for award certificates from reputable periodicals.
3. Ask whether or not substitutions are a problem. If the answer is yes, then you may want to dine elsewhere.
4. Talk to the maitre d' at the door. Is he a fresh college kid with an aloof nature, or is he a person whose opinions about food you would trust? If the maitre d' is impolite, or fails to provide what you consider to be courteous treatment, then leave the restaurant immediately.
5. Restaurants should be willing to display their menu outside or allow you to scan it in the foyer. Beware of menus with no prices because they will be astonishingly expensive. You should never eat in a very expensive restaurant unless you are confident in the quality of the food.

If you can't find suitable restaurants in your area, then we suggest you learn how to cook. Being your own best chef is an acquired skill, but with a little reading and a lot of practice you can master your kitchen and delight your imagination and lust for good cooking without having to pay the restaurant's overhead. The best snobs are also wonderful chefs, and knowing how to have small dinner parties is one of the real snob's true virtues.

Drinking should be an art form, not just a way to get loaded, at least if you are a real (and truly likeable) snob. Drinking is always a matter of personal taste, but if your taste is for Red Ripple on the rocks with a twist, then we can't help you. However, if you like what you drink, then it is your own business. If you gulp down what you order in time to order another before the waiter leaves the table, then you probably shouldn't drink in public. If drinking gives you a headache, then you probably shouldn't drink at all. We do not endorse drinking, because it can and does do bad things to otherwise good folks. On the other hand, some doctors recommend moderate imbibing for cardiac health, and for centuries "a wee sma' drappie" has kept the chill out of human bones.

Again, our basic advice is to try out some alternatives before deciding what you really like is Seven & Seven. In fact, it is our sincere belief that if you have to mask the taste of alcohol with sugary syrups and wild fruit flavors, you probably can't get into Heaven because surely the good Lord knows better!

Drinking is fun when it is done in moderation. Nothing can ruin a career as quickly as a drug problem, and alcohol is a very powerful drug.

A FINAL NOTE ON BECOMING A SNOB

We have tried to present a positive view of being a snob, which we could just as easily have called a "well-informed citizen," although that title didn't have the sex appeal of "snobbery." We believe that the successful, real snob is a person who cultivates her or his own tastes and is regarded by others as a source of reliable information on a variety of subjects and experiences. In the olden days this person was known as a "person of good character and breeding," or a "credible source," or, for those remnant Ciceronians among you, a "rhetorician." Truly this is the good person speaking well. . . .

There is the other side of snobbery, though. This is the image of the snob as constant critic of everybody and everything—the sayer of sarcastic remarks, the pretender to greatness, the wicked in word and deed. This image is not a favorable one, although there are many persons who believe that if you can say the most outrageous things about others, if you can insult with the best of them, then you must know something the rest of us don't know. Bull. This is the person who is a pest, a person whose only pleasures are those moments when he or she is able to put-down the present company, and somehow feel elevated by the experience. This is not snobbery, but *effrontery*. This is not virtue, but poor verisimiltude.

When you mature into a successful snob, likeable or not, there will be others who hold your knowledge and skills against you. These persons are known as "terminal middle managers," and should be avoided. There will be others who, as the Kinks used to say, are "dedicated followers of fashion" or fads, and their vicarious turn-ons are usually dangerous, momentary, and probably not worth the effort. In fact, as you develop your snob status, you will find that there are few people worthy of your friendship and time. Perhaps this is a sad reality, but on the other hand, the person who makes it in any organization chooses his or her company wisely.

Improving Your Snob I.Q., Part II

1. Where do the famous copulating pandas reside? What is the genetic heritage of the panda bear?
2. What is the worst turnpike in the nation? What is the best way to get through that state without having to use it? What is the major disadvantage of the alternate route?
3. Why is Jack Daniel's Distillery located in a dry county? At what age did Jack found the distillery, and how tall was he when he did it? What is the secret to making Jack Daniel's? What are the *three* labels Jack Daniel's is sold under?
4. Who is Carl Haas, and why should every classical music lover know his name?
5. Give three good reasons for entering southern California. Give two reasons for staying there longer than you have to. Now give one good reason for leaving it.

chapter six

FROM FIRST IMPRESSIONS TO PERFORMANCE REVIEWS

"To know a person, close your eyes and open your ears."
—TACITUS

"No one can make you feel inferior without your consent."
—ELEANOR ROOSEVELT

"Whatever ignominy or disgrace we have incurred, it is almost always in our power to reestablish our reputation."
—LA ROCHEFOUCALD

THE NATURE OF EVALUATION IN ORGANIZATIONS

In America we are guaranteed the freedom to learn what we are capable of learning, to speak what we believe to be the truth, and to act out the dictates of our individual consciousnesses. Although we hold these freedoms up as lights of wisdom to the world, we are also mindful of the responsibilities these freedoms incur. So it is that most of us, most of the time, obey the laws of our country and our organizations, show politeness and courtesy to others, and hope for a fair return on our investments in living, loving, and working.

One reason for our compliance with the laws of our nation or the rules that govern our behavior in organizations is we know that if we violate them we may be punished. We tend to act in the spirit of Sigmund Freud's timeless truth—to seek pleasure and avoid pain. So it is we enter a world in which evaluations of our behavior, our goals, and ourselves are a prominent, permanent part of our progress from cradle to grave. As a child we work for the attention and caring of our parents and siblings. In school we work for grades and for the respect of our peers. And when we enter the world of organizations and agencies, from Huntsville to Honolulu, our grades come in pay envelopes, and the respect we win from our peers comes in raises and promotions.

We keep seeking more respect, more money, and more power all the days of our lives. Getting them, however they are defined, means we are doing well, moving up, taking over. These are the symbols, real and ethereal, of our success in organizations, and as such represent evaluations of us made by others. Sometimes we get a cool, dispassionate review of our work at appraisal review time. Sometimes we receive passionate, spontaneous evaluations, reflected in our joy and anger about the people around us. Both of these evaluations are entered on our records. The cool evaluations find their way into our formal personnel records and are reflected in our increases in pay and position. The passionate evaluations become grist for the gossip mill, and also are reflected in our pay and promotions. These evaluations make up our reputations.

In this chapter, we discuss how you can keep track of how well you are doing in any organization. We show you how to watch the responses you get from others when you act, and how to monitor the talk you carry on with others. Next we suggest some ways you can influence the evaluations others make of you. Finally, we show you how your performance personality can be used to obtain more and better payoffs.

THE MEANING OF HUMAN BEHAVIOR: A PRAGMATIC INTRODUCTION

Evaluations begin with assessments of what behavior *means*. Consider the judgments you pass about others. What causes them?

What prompts you to think that Susan is a "smart, good-looking woman with a lot of potential," or that Sam is a "dumb, ugly, ruthless bureaucrat with nowhere to go and no reason to improve?" It is important to ask what prompts these evaluations of others because very often we assume "this is the way *everyone* sees them," or worse, we assume "this is the way they *are*." We tend to act as if our judgments were universal pronouncements, capable of gaining consensus among all rational adults.

Evaluations are individual assessments of the meanings and motives of other's *behavior*, based on conscious and unconscious comparisons of the other person with ourselves and with other persons we have known. For example, when you say "Susan is a smart, good-looking woman with a lot of potential" you may be suggesting as much about yourself as you are about Susan. You may think her "smart" because she agrees with you, or because she demonstrates the skills of argument (which you value); you may think she is "good-looking" because she fits your culturally derived model of attractiveness, or because she has commented on your own good looks, or because she is about as physically attractive as you think you are; and, you may think she "has a lot of potential" because you like her, or because if she succeeds you may be rewarded by her, or because she saved your precious behind once and you are forever in her debt. When you pass along these informal judgments about others, you are saying as much about yourself as you are about them.

Evaluations are always *comparative summaries* in which the self-esteem and values of the evaluator figure prominently in the assessment rendered. This is the reason why most organizations favor formal, objective performance appraisal reviews. Organizations have learned not to rely as heavily on informal, personal evaluations because of their inherent biases toward the evaluator. This does not mean personal opinions don't enter into formal reviews; it means most organizations know it is important to gain assessments of work done as well as how others have perceived your behavior while doing the work. Consider the following testimony.

Joan.

I worked in an office where sexual innuendo was commonplace, and I never thought anyone really took it seriously. I mean, you should hear some of the filthy jokes that we passed around. Anyway, my girlfriend Cathy used to say "Joan, you are *such* a slut" to me after I told a joke, and everyone would laugh. Then the trouble started. Men stared at my legs, my chest, looked longingly into my eyes, that sort of thing. I know I'm attractive, so I didn't pay any attention at first. But then the subtle propositions started, and that's when I got confused. Why me? Was it because I told some dirty jokes? Men do that sort of thing all the time and nobody thinks them bad or easy because of it. But it came to me that Cathy's "innocent" little statement and all that silly laughter was really just a cover for a reputation that I didn't deserve but was getting anyway. But I learned the lesson too late; during my first appraisal I was informed that my behavior was "distracting" to other workers. I knew what was meant. I only wish that I had known what was really going on before I was made a victim of it.[1]

Joan learned too late how important it is to monitor communication with others. Too often we discount the value of *talk*, especially casual talk exchanged with other employees, as sources of ongoing evaluations made about us. We tend to devalue the potential for talk to reveal meaning by stupidly clinging to the old maxim "Actions speak louder than words," or worse "Sticks and stones may break my bones, but words will never hurt me." Communication not only creates human relationships, it also provides data about them. To succeed in any organization requires an ability to monitor what is being said to you and about you.

Here is our guide to monitoring communication in evaluations made about you.

1. *Think before you speak:* This age-old wisdom is passed down from generation to generation for good reason—it is still true!

---

[1]Humor is a particular problem for women in any organization because they are not "supposed" to be profane. And when they are profane, men tend to see the profanity as a character trait.

Think about the *purpose* or *goal* for what you are about to say before you say it. If you can't identify the goal, chances are you have no good reason to speak.

2. *Consider talk to be how you exert influence and control over situations and others:* You are known by your words and deeds. You can exert influence over evaluations of yourself by monitoring the words you speak and the actions you perform in the presence of others. There is no such thing as "cheap talk." All talk is valuable because it provides information about you to persons who are in the information-processing business. Make sure you get a fair return for your investment by understanding how talk creates possibilities for judgments made about you.

3. *Pay attention to comments made about you, your work, and your relationships with others:* Listening is important because there is much information to be gained from it. You have to learn to be as interested in what others are saying as you are in what you say to them.

4. *Try to adapt your communication to the needs and expectations of others:* People tend to respond favorably to us when we exhibit concern for them, particularly when we can help them solve their problems or meet their expectations. This doesn't mean you should engage in therapy or sacrifice your goals and work to help someone else. It does mean you should try to figure out what people want from you and then determine whether or not you can or should deliver it. Also, after you have done something for someone else, seek feedback about how well you've met their expectations.

5. *Judge not, lest you too be judged:* Avoid the temptation to make informal evaluations of others in public. Remember, the rule of reciprocity usually holds true—if you pass judgment on the personality and work of others, then others may feel inclined to pass judgments about you.

6. *Be willing to modify your behavior:* Too often we believe that whatever we are doing, we are doing it correctly. It is always a good idea to seek feedback about your performance on the job and attempt to modify your actions based on the criticism or suggestions for change you receive.

7. *Avoid communicating with troubled persons, or with victims of the*

past: Guilt by association is a fact of organizational life. Choose whom you communicate with wisely. Avoid discussing marital or personal problems with coworkers, avoid associating with persons who want to tell you their woes. It is never wise to associate with rebels within the organization, or with persons who openly insult your peers, subordinates, or superiors. You will be evaluated on the quality of the company you seek and keep.

INFLUENCING JUDGMENTS ABOUT THE WORK YOU'VE DONE

Did you ever feel you weren't getting credit for the work you'd done? Have you ever seen someone you work with get a big raise and promotion and wondered why you didn't receive similar rewards? Have you ever found out that someone stole your idea and wondered what you could do about it? These are some of the symptoms of a very common problem. The problem is not knowing how to influence judgments about the work you've done, and the result of the problem may be that you lose an opportunity to advance your career and end up blaming someone else for something you should have done.

Read the last sentence in the preceeding paragraph again. The point is the only person you can rightfully blame for your own professional disappointments is *yourself*—not the other person who is rewarded in your place, not the organization for failing to recognize your worth, and certainly not the evaluation process that you may feel unfairly reviewed your work. The buck you want to pass begins and ends with you. You, and the responses you get from others, are the stuff your dreams and destinies are made of!!

If you assume that most of what is known and thought about you is contained in the words you speak and the actions you perform, then it is a curious notion indeed that somehow you will be rewarded solely on "your merits," or worse, "because everyone knows how valuable you really are." It is wishful thinking to believe you will be rewarded solely on your merits. No one knows your merits unless you tell them.

This doesn't mean you should walk around touting your accomplishments, nor does it mean that you should use every occasion to let others know just how hard you are working. Nobody likes a loudmouth braggart, and telling people how hard you are working only encourages them to believe you are either (a) showing off, or (b) too stupid to get the work done more economically. So the dilemma becomes how to influence judgments about your worth to the organization without appearing to be a self-centered, conceited little snot. You must learn to use talk *persuasively* to call your merits to the attention of those responsible for evaluating them. Consider the case of Gus:

Gus.

> I had to go see a shrink before I could tell somebody how good I was. I swear I was the best damned engineer at —————, and I never once got credit. Lou was always talking about his designs, and Linda was always bragging about her "price-saving options," and yet I did better designing and cost cutting than both of them put together! And furthermore, I kept working while they were talking. I never made idle chit-chat with the boss. I was too busy doing my job.

Gus's problem was he didn't have a *persuasion* plan. Think of persuasion as purposeful communication. It is purposeful because you have a plan, a strategy, and a way of carrying it out to obtain the goals you seek. To have a plan requires you to:

1. *Analyze your audience:* Aristotle once pointed out that "the fool persuades me with his reasons, the wise man with my own." Your attempts at persuading must always be directed at a particular audience. The question becomes, then, who do you need to persuade? Your peers, certainly, because you need their help to coordinate activities that will result in accomplishments. Your superior(s), naturally, because he or she will be responsible for evaluating the work you've done. But to think of these individuals in abstract terms, such as "peers," or "superiors," is to defeat your plan before you can implement it. You need to reduce the level of abstraction by carefully analyzing the *needs and expectations* of every mother's daughter and son among them. Consider your conversations with them to be information-seeking interviews, a time dur-

ing which you can explore their expectations of you and their preferred methods for carrying out assignments. Instead of engaging in conversations about the weather or other mindless tidbits of talk, ask questions about work-related issues and listen carefully to the answers they provide. Not only will you encourage your peers to see you as a serious professional person, you will also avoid the pitfalls of spontaneity that include untoward comments about others, spreading rumors or gossip you will later regret, and wasting time. When you meet with your superior, ask for directives and make sure you understand exactly what you are responsible for doing, how it is to be done, and when it is due. You may want to set up a periodic review of your progress and use these sessions to gain feedback about your work.

2. *Clearly define your goals:* As the old Chinese proverb has it: "If you don't know where you are going, any road will get you there." You need to know exactly what your goals are so you can map out a safe, efficient route. In part your goals will be determined by your talk with peers and superiors, and in part your goals will be selected by your own desire to accomplish tasks and build your professional image. Avoid vaguely stated goals such as "I want to be well liked"; instead identify those specific behaviors you could see in others that would signal their "liking" you. Avoid unrealistic goals such as "I want to be Vice-President of the Marketing Division before I'm 30"; instead focus on goals you can accomplish within six months or one year's time.

3. *Map out a basic strategy for reaching your goals and build in contingencies:* A large part of succeeding in any task is the ability to *organize* work so it can be accomplished in an orderly, systematic way. Think of this mapping out of a strategy as the creation of *order* in your work and in your life. Most successful individuals, from Ben Franklin to the person at the desk next to yours, recognize the value of *managing time*. If you don't have a regular schedule for carrying out the responsibilities of your life, you likely will always feel somewhat behind or depressed because of your failure to find time to do what you need to do (see Chapter Three on time and space management).

Your objectives must be clearly defined and you should have a preferred schedule for reaching them, but if something unexpected occurs, you also need *contingencies* to allow you to accomplish your goals using different strategies. Whom can you call to help you if something goes wrong? If the computer is down and you need desperately to use a computer, where else can you go to run your program? Remember: Strategies help you anticipate situations, but they do not prevent problems from happening. You must be able to demonstrate calm resourcefulness when times are tough if you are going to persuade anyone that you are as competent a professional as you claim to be.

4. *Keep accurate records of your progress:* You never know when your superior, who told you that you wouldn't have to give a status report until —————, may be replaced by someone who wants to know what is going on *right now*. Unless you've kept neat, careful records you will snatch defeat from the jaws of success. The organized person always has information. The few extra minutes each day you spend dictating or writing out your notes may save your hide if someone challenges the work you've done, or if for some reason a higher-up wants to review your progress. One additional advisory about keeping records: *Always be sure they are neatly typed, correctly spelled, and grammatically pure.* A person who doesn't care about spelling may not care about other small, but important details. And these days, with the availability of personal computers/word processors that check spelling, there is no good reason not to spell correctly. You will still need to go over your work, because these handy devices only catch about 85% of the errors.

5. *Use informal situations to your professional advantage:* Hardly a day goes by without at least a dozen people saying: "How are you doing?" Instead of saying "Fine, and you?" say "I'm doing quite well, actually, and my project is progressing better than I expected." (You must be sure your project *is* going better than expected if you make this claim.) Informal chatter is just that unless you use the opportunity to communicate your professional competence. However, you don't want to overplay your hand. Select the moments for these displays of image-building carefully. It helps if you carry a copy of your records on the project with you, so that if invited to discuss the wonderful progress you claim to be making, you can provide the necessary documentation.

6. *Actively seek feedback about your work:* If you submit a status report or give a formal presentation, ask your superior for a meeting to discuss his or her responses to it. Listen carefully to the reactions and if he or she requests additional information or changes, do exactly what is asked of you.

7. *Compliment others who work with you:* Everyone needs an occasional pat on the back or kind word. Because most tasks these days are accomplished by groups of people working together, it is important to present *group* work as the product of the group rather than as your own accomplishment. Advancement in virtually every professional category is based in part on the ability to demonstrate leadership, and leadership is a *group* activity. You can take credit for organizing and coordinating the group's activities, but you should always point out the individual contributions of group members when speaking with your superior. If your work group is well respected, you will all reap the rewards of work well done.

Knowing how to persuade is a useful and necessary skill in your professional repetoire of competencies. Norman Mailer once wrote a book whose title was *Advertisements for Myself*. The ability to advertise your competencies and accomplishments requires the skill of persuading all the audiences to whom you play. And for those few readers who may still doubt the need to persuade others in order to advance their careers, we remind them of the difference between the codfish and the hen.

> The codfish lays a million eggs, the little hen but one.
> But the codfish doesn't cackle, to tell us when she's done.
> So we despise the codfish, while the little hen we prize,
> Which indicates to thoughtful minds, it pays to advertise.

THE PERFORMANCE PERSONALITY AND APPRAISAL REVIEWS

There are at least four different ways to approach a performance appraisal review. Think of each one as *attitudes* toward your performance over the year.

1. *The performance review as a time of crisis and regret:* If you have serious misgivings about what might transpire during your performance review, then chances are you will approach the situation as a major crisis. You may express regret for not having accomplished your tasks as well as you should have, and you may offer explanations for your poor performance—personal difficulties, family trouble, lack of adequate resources, lack of time, misjudgment of the task and its requirements, or general *ennui*. Worse, you will probably *look terrible* during the time of the appraisal process because your nerves will feel as if they are being worn on the outside of your skin, and your sleepless nights will show on your face, especially around the eyes. If this sounds like you, then brace yourself for a nonsoothing but practical bit of advice: *Begin looking for another job immediately!* If *you* feel your performance is poor and you are ruining your health worrying about it, then chances are your performance has been below standard and you will have a very difficult time regaining the respect of your superiors. A poor performance review remains on your record. Ask your supervisor for a conference *prior to* the appraisal, explain your problem, and see whether or not she or he might be willing to help you find employment elsewhere. You may be able to prevent a poor performance review by anticipating it and moving around it, but you can't do anything about it after the fact.

2. *The performance review as a long headache accompanied by extreme anxiety:* If you worry about the performance appraisal process despite feeling that you have done a good job with assignments, then chances are you are forcing yourself to suffer from anxiety without having to. This approach may be today's standard—most persons fear what they do not know, especially when a pay raise may be involved. Your behavior will signal distress. Sleepless nights produce the look of sleepless nights; abuse of alcohol, nicotine, or other drugs show on the surface of the skin what they are doing in your central nervous system. If you *look like you are about to be made a victim of the appraisal process*, then chances are you encourage others to believe your performance has been less than standard. When this is *not* the case, then you represent a tragic irony in a business suit. You want to give the appearance of confidence prior to the

review, you want to inspire others (especially your superiors) to believe that you aren't worried because you have nothing to worry about.

3. *The performance review as a time of laughter and forgetting:* If you approach the performance review as an end to the old, haggard times and troubles that characterized the previous year's work, as an opportunity to begin fresh with a positive outlook for the year ahead, then the review process will not disturb you in the ways it is designed to. In fact, you may inspire distrust or anger in your superiors because of your nonchalant attitude toward what most persons in management believe to be a serious situation. *You* may want to laugh about the past and forget the difficult times, but *your superior* may want to offer suggestions about how to overcome those difficulties, or investigate those rough experiences for symptoms and causes of deeper problems. Your comic responses may only suggest that you are insincere about improving your performance, or that you really don't care what happened or how difficulties can be overcome. Beyond these appearances, you may also be communicating your disapproval of the status differences that naturally separate superiors and subordinates. Hence, from this time on, you may be perceived as a troublemaker or a threat to authority.

4. *The performance review as an opportunity to negotiate objectives, ways and means of reaching them, and to demonstrate professional competencies:* If this is your approach to the appraisal review process, congratulations, because you have what we consider to be the best possible attitude toward the situation. If you are confident about your accomplishments during the review period, convinced that your dealings with others have been fair and equitable, and see past achievements as grounds for increasing your responsibilities and status for the coming year, then you ought to be able to use the performance appraisal process to your persuasive advantage. Plan for your interview by reminding yourself of your accomplishments, by outlining what you want to achieve for the next review period, and thinking through what resources you need to achieve your new objectives. Go into the interview prepared to negotiate the future, not simply review the past.

Now let's examine the performance review process for a basic understanding of how the evaluations can take place, and what you can do to prepare yourself for them.

The Review Process

Most organizations formally evaluate performance on a yearly basis, although some companies prefer more frequent appraisals (e.g., quarterly, semiannually). The performance review, in theory, is an opportunity for the organization to examine the work of each one of its divisions or components, and each individual's contributions to the overall performance of the firm.

It is important for your boss to have good and bad in any review. If all is well, then top management becomes suspicious and there is less reason to reward the middle manager—after all, why reward the tender of the flock when the flock is managing itself? So it is middle management's practical responsibility to seek out demons and exorcise them in a way that will attract favorable attention from their superiors.

As we have pointed out, if you have consciously monitored your behavior and responses to your performance over the review period, then you should have little to fear. You will know what to expect. If not, then you are a candidate for unwanted surprises.

Either way, the review process from your point of view will consist of the same steps: (1) you will be asked to provide details about your work during the performance review period (usually this will be in the form of a written report with an appended résumé); (2) your report will be read by your superior(s), compared with other similar reports, and a formal written evaluation of your performance will be recorded—usually this includes an "objective" numerical assessment using a standard rating form and a "subjective" narrative assessment using whatever words the superior feels are appropriate; and (3) you will be asked to submit to a formal performance appraisal interview with your immediate superior, who will review your report, his or her appraisal, and discuss your future objectives with you. After the third step is completed, you will have an opportunity to signal your agreement with the performance review (usually by signing the document provided with your written review), or to file a grievance with the personnel office if you think you have been treated unfairly.

Each one of these steps is critically important because in the world according to business *success means never having to say you are sorry during appraisal time.* Let's see what you can do to improve your chances for success during the appraisal review.

Making the Appraisal System Work for You

Your first opportunity to make the appraisal system work for you is in the construction of your report to your supervisor or superior. You have to learn how to account for the work you've done. You have to write the report in a clear, concise, and persuasive way, using a format appropriate to the needs and expectations of your reader. And you have to be able to reveal your strengths without overly inflating your ego. Here is what you need to do:

1. *Collect your evidence and organize it:* Most persons do not make the most of an appraisal opportunity because they do not spend adequate time researching what they have actually accomplished over the year. You need to have information about (a) your assigned duties, including any formal written documents that you created or used to complete your assignments; (b) any extra duties you formally assumed, and any records of what you did while working on them; (c) any projects on which you helped out, but did not receive formal credit; and (d) any letters of appreciation, congratulations, or merit you received over the course of the appraisal period. These sources of information should then be organized according to (a) *chronology*, or from the beginning of the appraisal period to the end of it; (b) *success of the assignment from the perspective of your boss*; and (c) *demonstrations of leadership ability on your part*, including the number and kind of group meetings you chaired, the consulting favors you did for other persons on other projects, and any formal written and/or oral presentations you made to superiors. What you want to be able to demonstrate is a year during which time you progressively accomplished more

goals and demonstrated increased sensitivity to leadership obligations.

2. *Plan a persuasive strategy for your report:* You don't just want your appraisal report *read;* you want it to have *maximum impact on the reader.* Many persons fail to make persuasive use of the opportunity to put into writing their accomplishments; they just write whatever they can remember, in whatever style seems appropriate for the document. They fail to remind themselves that *form and content are interdependent structures*!! How the document is written and organized will influence the reader's perceptions of its content. For this reason, you should make use of a persuasive document design. The following persuasive document design provides a sentence-by-sentence account of exactly what you should include, and in the order of the material presented.

All formal reports should contain a *Beginning* consisting of four distinct statements:

1. A *statement/question designed to gain the attention of the reader* [e.g., short narrative, important question, startling statistic, or other similar inducements, such as: How can one year's work be reduced to a two-page account of assignments and accomplishments?]
2. *Thesis* or purpose sentence [e.g., "This report will summarize my work activities for the appraisal period 15 March 198___–15 March 198___."]
3. *Preview* of the internal contents/divisions of the document [e.g., "First, I will describe my assignment with the Trojan Horse project; second, I will discuss my accomplishments with the technical staff; and finally, I will summarize my thinking about my work during this appraisal period."]
4. *Statement of inducement* pointing out to the reader what she/he will know as a result of completing this document [e.g., "As a result of reading this report, you will be better able to assess my progress for ——————— this year."]

All formal reports should contain a *Middle* consisting of major claims [statements you want your reader to remember], evidence in support of those claims [e.g., examples, statistics, testimony of other persons, etc.], and a transition to the next major claim:

1. State your *First Major Claim* [e.g., "I completed all assigned duties on the Trojan Horse project on or before schedule."]

2. State *evidence* in support of your claim [e.g., "My assignments included gathering all the financial data concerning the construction of the horse, projecting a five-year cost schedule on predictions of market value, and coordinating all research efforts with members of the technical staff. This work culminated in a technical report [dated 1 February 1985] submitted to all personnel assigned to the project. For completing this assignment two months ahead of schedule I received a letter of commendation from Freda Wiltmier, Director of the Trojan Horse Project. See Appendix A for letter dated 12 February 1985."]

3. Provide a *transition* to your next major claim [e.g., "Now that I have described my duties on the project, I will discuss major achievements in the areas of leadership and coordination of technical staff members assigned to me for the project."]

4. State your *second major claim* [e.g., "I mastered the ability to provide cogent directives and assignment schedules for technical staff members on the Trojan Horse Project."]

5. Provide your *evidence* in support of the second claim [e.g., "This task was accomplished by holding a staff project meeting on each Monday morning at 8:30 A.M. For each meeting I circulated a formal agenda and requested that any amendments or proposed changes be discussed with me prior to the meeting. During the meeting I instituted standard agenda to guide work on the project, and provided instruction to staff members about the use of the standard agenda procedures. As a result of each staff member completing assigned work on or before deadlines, we were able to provide a status report on 15 December 1984 and a final project report on 1 February 1985. I believe the hard work and dedication of my staff enhanced my ability to provide leadership on this project. Upon completing the final project report I asked each member of the technical staff to complete an assessment of the group's work and my leadership skills. I have taken the liberty of attaching the results of that survey to this appraisal report. See Appendix B.]'

6. Provide a transition to your third major claim [e.g., "In the next paragraph I summarize my work during this appraisal period and provide a brief synopsis of my major goals for the next appraisal period."]

7. State your *third major claim* [e.g., "I believe my accomplishments during this appraisal period, particularly my work on the horse project, clearly demonstrate my ability to go above and beyond routine duties provided by my formal job description."]

8. Provide *evidence* for the third major claim [e.g., "My ability to complete all assigned duties on or before due dates, my handling of the interpersonal and task-related difficulties of the project, and my guidance of the technical staff toward completion of the project all provide support for my claim of leadership abilities. I am ready for more challenging assignments."]

9. Provide a *transition* to your review and conclusion [e.g., "Hence, my goals for the upcoming appraisal period include the ability to seek out newer, more challenging projects requiring my professional and leadership capabilities."]

After you have completed the internal divisions of your document, you are ready to write your *Review and Conclusion*:

1. *Review* the major claims you have advanced in the middle of your report [e.g., "This appraisal report summarizes my assignments and accomplishments for the year. I have provided brief accounts of my work on the Trojan Horse Project and my accomplishments directing the work of the technical staff. I concluded with a statement expressing interest in assuming more challenging duties during the upcoming year."]

2. *Conclude* your report by returning to the attention-gaining material [e.g., "At the beginning of this report I asked the question "How can one year's work be reduced to a two-page account of assignments and accomplishments?" As a result of reading this account I believe you now have the necessary facts concerning my work at ―――――. My hope is that this information will open a dialogue between us about my assignments for next year. Thank you for this opportunity."]

3. *Prepare for your appraisal interview:* In the second chapter we discussed the importance of preparing for *any* interview. The preparation for an appraisal interview is similar to the preparation you must complete for a job interview. First, you need to research the organization, and especially its goals for the appraisal process. Second, you need to analyze your superior or supervisor—the one conducting your appraisal. What questions will she or he likely ask? What kinds of support can you offer? How can you embellish what is contained in your written report? What questions can you ask to clarify how your review is proceeding, and what your chances are for getting the assignment you want? What should you wear to enhance your professional image? What are you going to say if your supervisor (a) argues *against* any of the points you

A Sample Appraisal Report

TO: Ms. Mary Bogar, Chief
        Special Projects Division
        Creative Games, Inc.

FROM: R.F. HOWARD

RE: APPRAISAL REPORT

How can one year's work be reduced to a two-page account of assignments and accomplishments? This report will summarize my work activities for the appraisal period 15 March 1984 to 15 March 1985. First, I will describe my assignment with the Trojan Horse project; second, I will discuss my accomplishments with technical staff; and finally, I will summarize my thinking about my work during this appraisal period. As a result of reading this report, you will be better able to assess my progress for Creative Games, Inc., this year.

I completed all assigned duties on the Trojan Horse Project on or before schedule. My assignments included gathering all the financial data concerning the construction of the horse, projecting a five-year cost schedule based on predictions of market value, and coordinating research efforts with members of the technical staff. This work culminated in a technical report (dated 1 February 1985) submitted to all personnel assigned to the horse project. For completing this assignment two months ahead of schedule, I received a letter of commendation from Freda Wiltmier, Director of the Trojan Horse Project (see Appendix A for letter dated 12 February 1985). Now that I have described my duties on the horse project, I will discuss major achievements in the areas of leadership and coordination of technical staff members assigned to me for the project.

I mastered the abilities to provide cogent directives and assignment schedules for technical staff members on the Trojan Horse Project. This task was accomplished by holding a staff project meeting each Monday morning at 8:30 A.M. For each meeting I circulated a formal agenda and requested that any amendments or proposed changes be discussed with me prior to the meeting. During the meeting I instituted standard agenda to guide work on the project, and provided instruction to staff members about the use of the standard agenda procedures. As a result of each staff member completing assigned work on or before deadlines, we were able to provide a status report on 15 December 1984 and a final project report on 1 February 1985. I believe the hard work and dedication of my staff enhanced my ability to provide leadership on this project. Upon completing the final project report I asked each member of the technical staff to fill out an assessment of the group's work and my leadership skills. I have taken the liberty of attaching the results of that survey to this appraisal report (see Appendix B). In the next paragraph, I summarize my work during this appraisal period and provide a brief synopsis of my major goals for the next appraisal period.

I believe my accomplishments during the appraisal period, particularly my work on the horse project, clearly demonstrate my ability to go above and beyond routine duties provided by my formal job description. My ability to complete all assigned duties on or before due dates, my handling of the interpersonal and task-related difficulties on the project, and my guidance of the technical staff toward completion of the project two months ahead of schedule all provide support for my claim of leadership abilities. I am ready for a more challenging assignment. Hence, my goals for the upcoming appraisal period include the ability to seek out newer, more challenging projects requiring my professional and leadership capabilities.

This appraisal summarizes my assignments and accomplishments for the year. I have provided brief accounts of my work on the Trojan Horse Project and my accomplishments directing the work of the technical staff. I concluded with a statement expressing interest in assuming more challenging duties during the upcoming year. At the beginning of this report I asked the question "How can one year's work be reduced to a two-page account of assignments and accomplishments?" As a result of reading this account I believe you now have the necessary information concerning my work with Creative Games, Inc. My hope is that this information will open a dialogue between us about my assignments for next year.

Thank you for this opportunity.

Cordially,

R. F. Howard

R.F. Howard

provide in your formal report, or (b) blocks your progress in the organization by denying you the assignment you feel you deserve? Thinking through these issues before facing them can provide you with ways and means of overcoming possible objections and persuasively obtaining your initial objectives.

4. *Use the appraisal interview to gain information about your standing in the organization:* Don't think that all that can be gained from the appraisal process is a raise or a promotion. Far more important is the information you get about your superior's perceptions of you as an employee and as a person. Be alert to verbal and nonverbal cues that communicate his or her *real* meaning. Remember to ask questions to clarify (a) abstract statements, (b) unclear goals for the upcoming year, and (c) raises or promotions (if any). Be a good, attentive listener and you gain the important strategic advantage.

5. *Negotiate for what you feel you deserve and want:* Too often people forget that the appraisal interview is an event with *four* legs. You aren't just there to receive information; you are also there to provide sound reasons and arguments for what you think you deserve. If the raise doesn't seem large enough, ask why not. If the promotion is not forthcoming, seek advisories about what you can do to improve your chances for next year. If you don't seem to be receiving the kind of assignment you have worked for, then provide good reasons for getting it.

6. *If you don't get what you want, don't make a scene:* Careers are ruined in swift instances where emotional displays replace sound reasoning and humility. If you don't receive the appraisal you feel you deserve, you can almost always file a grievance with the appropriate office. Before using that channel, however, you should try to gain information about why you are being denied what you feel you deserve. Maybe the company is having financial trouble that will clear up in the near future. Maybe your supervisor doesn't have all the information she or he needs to justify giving you a raise or promotion—maybe you need to provide that information. Perhaps rumors and gossip have been spread about you that you need to check out. Whatever the cause of your disappointment, you need to check it out before acting on impulses that may reveal you in an even more negative light.

7. *Keep accurate records of your appraisals:* One form of leaving a

"paper trail" is the copying and filing of all documents relating to your tenure with an organization. The numerical rating scale, the reports, the appended letters, memos, and technical documents, any grievances, and so on, should be kept forever. You never know when you will need them.

AFTER THE APPRAISAL: ON BECOMING A SUPERSTAR, A WONDERWOMAN, A GOLDEN BOY, AND OTHER WAYS OF SAYING YOU ARE DOING WELL

We want to end this chapter on a positive note. We will assume your performance personality paid off during the appraisal process, and you have been told your dreams of stardom are going to come true.

One common problem confronting rising stars in any organization is how to tell your less fortunate peers about your success. In movies this scene is usually played out in a sudden burst of enthusiasm by the hero or heroine, and applauded by all those assembled admirers who didn't fare as well in their appraisals but who are willing to give you your just rewards.

Unfortunately, most of us do not live in movies, nor do movies usually depict what really happens when success happens. Furthermore, unless your promotion brings with it the opportunity to reward your supporting cast, *your achievements* may inspire jealousy, hatred, envy, and brownnosing instead of applause. You may find living with success is as painful, perhaps even more painful, than coping with failure.

Another problem may be that you don't know how to reward yourself and those closest to you when you do succeed. Many persons report that big promotions seem anticlimatic—they literally do not know what to do to mark the event. Listen to Paul:

Paul.

When I was promoted I was so happy I didn't know what to do with myself. I called my wife, but she was having a bad day, and my success only pointed out the difference between her work situation and my own. I called my parents, and they were properly proud, but they always *expected* me to do well, so I was only confirming an assumption they held. My co-workers were congratulatory in ways that communicated to me their lack of genuine interest, except for Bob, who too clearly hoped that I would put in a good word for him. So I sat in my chair at the office for a while, and then, with nothing else to do, got back to work. The whole thing was depressing, when you consider the responses I got from others.

Our identities are shaped by the responses we get from others. When we are successful, and others don't treat us differently, our identities can suffer. We may get the feeling that we have been rewarded, but *Big Deal*! And all too often, these symbolic let-downs from friends, lovers, and family turn what ought to be a major victory into a sullen occasion.

Don't let this happen to you!

Part of our motivation for succeeding is based on the desire to have the special feeling that arises from knowing we've done well. If the feeling becomes associated with negative responses from our colleagues, our families, or our friends, we may not try as hard to succeed next time. Or worse, we may turn against those closest to us, thus further dividing ourselves from those whose responses matter the most to us. When we conducted our study of friendship, we were surprised to discover how often promotions end friendships. The general sentiment seemed to be success suggests a new difference exists between the friends, and that difference often proves insurmountable because of the tensions it creates for the relationship. Furthermore, we discovered successful spouses often cast off their partners, forgetting, as it were, the importance of *their* part in the drama.

Success can feel successful if it is approached modestly, and with full appreciation of those who have helped make the success possible. As good as *you* may feel when the promotion is announced, you need to help make others feel good about it too. This doesn't "just happen," as natural consequence of the event. It requires the successful person to actively induce cooperation among those who contributed to the event.

One way to do this is to *let others ask you how your performance review turned out* before announcing your success to them. If we walk around blowing our own horn, we appear egotistical, and no one likes to reward an egoist. On the other hand, if we wait long enough for others to inquire about how well we have done, we have a situation in which modest assessments of our review can be fully appreciated. Put simply: Wait for others to create the exigence for your response.

A second useful and satisfying way to feel rewarded for your success is to throw a party—have a celebration *for those persons who contributed to your achievement*. Notice how we worded the last sentence? You are *not* throwing a party for *yourself*; rather, you are throwing a party for those persons who helped you become successful. You should be the host or hostess for the occasion, not the person waited on or catered to. Probably the only time when you can have a party in your own honor without seeming to be a snob is upon the occasion of your retirement. Even then, it should be organized by those persons who feel it is an appropriate showing of appreciation for you. To have a party for yourself is to draw attention to your gluttonous pride.

Finally, you need to "keep on keepin' on." Achieving success only increases your responsibilities, makes greater demands on your time and freedom. You can't pause for a week or two unless you schedule a vacation. You need to acquire a process-orientation to succeeding. This will encourage you to view present successes as small steps leading to greater rewards in the future. But the point is not to "stop" just because you've won the first battle. There is still much work to be done.

Maintain an objective perspective on your own accomplishments. You may be a superstar for XYZ Corporation, the pride of Martinsburg, West Virginia, the best advertising copywriter in Phoenix, or the consensus genius of systems analysis in Houston, but who are you to the rest of the world? Even best-selling authors have to pay yearly dues for their American Express cards, and former major-league ballplayers understand all-too-well how quickly fans forget.

Improving Your Appraisal I.Q.

1. Let's say you are a supervisor or manager, and your task is to come up with the best, fairest, and most comprehensive appraisal review system for your organization. What would you do? Where would you begin? Would you design an appraisal review form with questions such as "How well did this person perform the assigned tasks?" Try to assign number values to each person you supervise, and then add up the scores. The top person gets the promotion, the above-average people get the bonuses, and the rest get cost-of-living increases, except for the really low ones, who get the axe, right? How equitable is this system? Do numbers really account for effort? Perseverance? Integrity? Compassion? Should these human values have any place in an appraisal review?

2. Okay. Now turn it around. Let's say the amazing appraisal system you developed is going to be used on *you*. Now do you want some way to evaluate those human values you just discarded? How can you explain this change of mind? Can it be that you want to be treated sympathetically by your boss? If so, what have you done lately to justify such treatment? If not, how can you be so sure your task performance will be the object of your boss's evaluations?

3. Answer this question truthfully: Do you really want your boss to evaluate your performance? If your answer is yes, then what persuasive strategies have you used to warrant your confidence? If your answer is no, then why is it no? What do you think she or he will *really* be evaluating? Or is that just an excuse you are using to cover poor performances? Be honest. No one but you is reading this page.

4. Are you sure you can handle the stress of becoming, and being, successful? What makes you think so? What about your spouse? What about your friends? How will they deal with you when you make it to the corner office at the top? More importantly, how will *you* deal with them as you rise?

chapter seven
TO ERR IS HUMAN

"Many is the word that only keeps you guessin'."

—ANONYMOUS

"If a man will begin with certainties, he will end with doubts;
but if he will be content to begin with doubts, he shall end in
certainties."

—FRANCIS BACON

"In the game of life anyone can win, unless there is a second
entry."

—THE AUTHORS

INTRODUCTION

A brilliant blue sky the color of a robin's eggs gives an illusion of
perfection. It is September, just after the autumn equinox, and it is
an unseasonably cool 75 degrees at midday. There is a slight
breeze, nothing to warn you. Five more hours until the weekend
begins, and the dead weight at the bottom of your gut seems like
the last load of the work week, you can almost feel it slipping away
like Friday. What could go wrong?

Just then, at the moment when your cares seem imaginary and there is the promise of a memorable weekend at least equal to the kind they show on televised beer commercials, the dam breaks, everything hits the fan, all hell breaks loose, and you are suddenly, irrevocably, in the grinder. Your boss, who only this morning exchanged kind words with you in the coffee room, threatens your job security in no uncertain terms. Your friends pretend they don't know you. Your secretary has the afternoon off. And your in-laws from Pennsylvania are arriving for their first visit at three o'clock,.

You have finally blown it, screwed up royally. The right thing is exactly the wrong thing, the excellent plan your promotion is riding on turns into a chaotic chorus of late-blooming mistakes, and there isn't anyone to blame for it except yourself. Now what do you do? How does the performance personality save face in times of crisis?

The theme of this chapter is how to deal with crises. This chapter is about how to identify what is going wrong and how to figure out what, if anything, you can do about it. It is a chapter about strategy and reflective thought and the cruel realities of antecedent conditions and consequent effects. It deals with common screw ups that plague everybody in every job in every company. It may become your survival manual.

THE DEADLY MYTH OF EFFORT

One of the harshest realities of working life is *nobody pays off on effort*. When you were a student you could sometimes get away with second rate work by whining to your teacher, "but I worked *so hard*, I put in hours and hours and hours on it." In contemporary organizations no one cares how many hours you put in on it, or how hard you worked, only whether or not you accomplished your assigned task on time.

The myth of effort is deadly. When you hear someone complain about their "hard work," you are hearing a plea for diminished responsibility. The logic is simple and silly: If I work hard, what I produce, no matter what its quality or quantity, should be enough to get by. People charged with criminal acts who plead "diminished responsibility" usually spend a long time in a mental hospital if they are acquitted, and an even longer time in jail if they are found guilty. In organizations people who work hard and let everybody know about it usually don't last very long. They are told their hard work would be better appreciated elsewhere.

Effort is assumed. Hard work is assumed. But getting the job done is what counts. Consider the following two ways of saying essentially the same thing. First, "I want you to know I worked all weekend on this crap, day and night, day and night. Didn't even get to take a break the whole time. Imagine that. So I finished it on time. So what? I wasted my weekend doing it. I'd better get some consideration around here from now on." Or you could say: "I put in two solid days and nights over the weekend, but you know what? I *finished* it. The work really paid off." Now, if *you* were the boss, which statement would you respect? Which person would you reward?

Research supports the idea of equity in organizations. The person who works all weekend to complete an important assignment, and who doesn't complain about it, is *less* likely to draw an overtime assignment again because it is clear the boss "owes you one." On the other hand, the person who does the same work over the weekend, and complains about it is *more* likely to draw another overtime assignment because *the complaint reduces the inequity*. In other words, when you complain you make it harder on yourself.[1]

Now that we have discussed the myth of effort, we will consider the philosophy of impairment.

THE PHILOSOPHY OF IMPAIRMENT

In any organization there are ordinary screw-ups and problems that lead to impairments. An impairment is a organizational prob-

---

[1] Of course there are supervisors who will overwork the noncomplainers because they "don't want to hear about it" from those who do complain, but these bosses are rarer than you might imagine. They also tend not to last very long because organizations will, at all costs, find ways to reduce inequity, reward talent, and punish the harmdoers.

lem that must be overcome if the organization is to prosper. To find an impairment you need to look for (a) something that should have happened that didn't happen, or (b) something that shouldn't have happened that did. These two sources of impairment are important to recognize because they allow you to locate the problem. Once you locate the problem, you can decide whether or not you should turn your hand to make it right. We say "decide" because there are some impairments you should stay away from—if the computer is down and you know nothing about repairing it, then stay away! If you aren't part of the solution, the old saying goes, you are part of the problem.

The first issue is to locate the impairment, otherwise known as finding out what happened. Simple and straightforward as this advice is, it is often the most easily overlooked. Persons who find themselves in an impaired situation tend to react emotionally. "Oh my cosmic God!" they scream, repeating the call for divine intervention until their mouths dry, "Oh my God, my God, my God . . . !" These are the broken records, the persons who can do nothing because they are stuck in the groove of emotion.

The performance personality does not react emotionally to impairments. Instead, the performance personality looks for the problem. To *act* is to come to *know*. You should act by asking questions designed to locate what happened. Did an order fail to get shipped? Did the order not arrive on schedule? Isn't there enough money to meet the payroll? Did the sales manager arrive for the presentation in Dallas only to find her display materials were waiting in Amarillo? Does the competition have a new program or product that is driving ours out of the market? Did some fanatic group raise a protest over our advertising campaign? Did the television show we sponsored fail to get the target ratings? Did the ad in Sunday's paper provide the wrong price?

Once you have found out what happened, the next question is what was its effect? What will be the likely consequences if the existing condition is allowed to continue? What will happen if whatever was supposed to happen does not, in fact, occur? What will be the result if the problem is not addressed? Sometimes you can examine a problem and discover it has a one time negative consequence (which may only require an apology), with no future effects. However, if you find out the impairment will result in future negative consequences, then you need to begin resolving the problem.

The third issue concerns whether the visible, identifiable impairment is a *symptom* or a *cause* of a more general, more widespread problem. If it is a symptom, then you may remove the impairment completely only to discover it was not the real problem. If it is a cause, then if you remove it you may solve the problem neatly.

Organizations often see symptoms and causes in direct relation to *persons*. The impairment becomes a reason to blame someone, or to fire someone else. As a person in charge, you need to be able to make distinctions between persons who *cause* problems, and problems that exist regardless of the persons tending to them. You also need to distinguish between symptoms that are revealed in the poor performance or impairments of a particular group or person, and symptoms that go deeper than the group or person involved. This is a necessary executive skill, and one that requires careful, reflective, and creative thought. It is the weak leader who blames the troops for a fault in the plan. Basically, there are six common sources of impairments.

1. *Organizational goals:* Sometimes organizations can't accomplish their stated objectives because they are seeking the wrong objectives. Many small home computer firms in the early 1980s suffered from this impairment. They entered the market with a particular product and the goal of capturing a "significant" share of the market. They backed their estimates with figures drawn from *current* market conditions, which often did not take into account the introduction of many other new firms seeking the same significant share. The result is well known. Many firms bit the corporate dust because their objectives were unobtainable.

2. *Quality of the product or service:* "Quality" has become Job 1 across the American auto industry despite the fact that Ford is the only manufacturer to use the slogan. The reason for this "new" emphasis on the quality of the product is simple: The Japanese,

French, and German imports pointed out the impairment to the American public. Whether or not there actually *was* a problem with the quality of American autos was not the issue—the point was an impairment with which millions of Americans could easily agree was pointed out and had to be addressed unless our manufacturers would go "belly up." However, improving the quality of a product or service has consequences any owner of a vintage Studebaker will gladly demonstrate— planned obsolescence must be replaced with new strategies of gaining annual income from sales. Japanese manufacturers accomplish this by introducing new products every year, French and German manufacturers charge considerably more for the servicing of their products.

The auto industry is not the only industry to be concerned with the quality of a product or service. Many firms now understand the importance of "customer satisfaction," and will go out of their way to provide it. Usually this means increasing the price of the product or service, or decreasing the advertising budget, but the better payoff in the long run is the new gamble.

3. *Changing market conditions or target audiences:* Conditions do change, and so do the markets. For example, many of the "Drug Counseling Centers," which grew up in the 1960s and early 1970s, had to be renamed "Drug *and* Alcohol Centers" as the clientele and existing market conditions changed. Furthermore, as newer and better research underscored the fact that many spouse and child abusers were "ordinary, upstanding citizens" in every other respect, new advertising campaigns aimed at the middle classes were needed.

Changing conditions are a fact of business life. Unless you are a mortician or a seller of Bibles, liquors, or soaps, there are few constants in your market. For this reason many consultants believe the most important branch of any organization is its strategic planning group responsible for keeping up with changes, predicting them when possible, and creating them in either case.

4. *Administrative maladies:* Administrative problems are serious impairments to any organization. For one thing, they occur at the top, and tend to trickle down through the ranks, like bad economic

policies. For another thing, they tend to focus on personalities and power, despite the obvious attempts to identify issues and decisions that went awry.[2]

The problem of administration is compounded by levels of management between the top decision makers and the persons responsible for carrying out the directives. Top managers, themselves struggling for power, may "seize the day," and confuse things. Middle managers, who must interpret directives, assign work, and supervise the supervisors, may apply their own logics to decisions made at the top and further confuse things. And supervisors must find some way to get the work done, regardless of whether or not it is the same work originally intended by the top managers or executives. Throughout the administrative hierarchies of any organization are communication breakdowns and inconsistencies, and the performance personality needs to understand that the best way to remove impairments might be to examine the flow of information for distortions.

5. *Personnel and managerial styles:* People are different, despite the fact most organizations tend to treat them similarly. Hence, one source of impairment may be clashes in style, or ways and means of carrying out directives.[3] These basic personality or style issues are further aggravated by issues of personnel *selection*.

Inability to match the proper person hired for the necessary job can seriously interfere with organizational operations. Companies that hire stenographers when they need word processing operators may find themselves with a cadre of loyal and competent personnel who no longer have anything to do. With recent advances in office technology, new problems arise. Companies who are forced to replace old personnel with new personnel equipped with the latest computer skills will inevitably make the older, less skilled employees uneasy. When the inequities begin to show

[2]See J.K. Benson, "Innovation and Crisis in Organizational Analysis," *Sociological Quarterly*, 18 (1977), 3–16; see also P.K. Tompkins, "Functions of Communication in Organizations," in C.C. Arnold and J.W. Bowers (Eds.), *Handbook of Rhetorical and Communication Theory* (Boston: Allyn & Bacon, 1984).

[3]See S. O'Connell, *The Manager as Communicator* (New York: Harper & Row, 1979).

themselves work suffers, and personnel-based impairments are never easy to resolve.

A final issue related to personnel and managerial styles concerns the singular issue of women and men. Women and men are different in their approaches to situations, people, and in their communicative styles.[4] Exhaustive research indicates that male attitudes toward female employees are as deeply rooted in cultural norms as they are in desire for corporate performance. The woman who steps out of these cultural standards jeopardizes how her work will be viewed, and unfortunately, there does not appear to be any easy answer to the dilemma. Females who rise in organizations do tend to either adopt traditional male managerial styles (authoritative, directive, sometimes insensitive or dispassionate), or use their physical assets to personal advantage. In either case, they tend to alienate other females and threaten males, thus separating themselves from the necessary social contacts so necessary for organizational success. Of course, this is not always the case. There are organizations that reward competence over sex appeal, and do not favor male managerial styles. Hopefully, more organizations will move in this enlightened direction in the near future.

6. *Fiscal impairments:* Discovery of fiscal problems is almost as complicated as solving them. It is fairly easy to say "we don't have enough money," but finding out how to gain more money or use it more efficiently is all too often an insurmountable problem. Borrowing means paying it back with interest. Cutting back the operation usually means laying off workers and causing distress signals throughout the organization. Expanding the stock means giving over greater control to the stockholders, who will, in return for their investment, require more profits than current operations can usually support. If you discover fiscal impairments in your organization, you will have to decide very quickly whether or not you can help bail them out of the crisis, (or risk losing your job and credibility when your efforts to do so fail), or find another job with a more financially solvent company. Money *is* the bottom line. Any com-

---

[4]See J. C. Pearson, *Gender and Communication* (Dubuque, Iowa: William C. Brown, 1984).

pany in serious financial difficulty (unless a government loan can be arranged) will retain the mediocre employees and lose the sharp ones. Which one you will be is the question.

These six common sources of impairment explain where to look when things go wrong, but they do not explain what you should do. In the following sections we examine various strategies to use when you find yourself in the middle of a serious hassle.

Improving Your Impairment I.Q.

1. When was the last time you could honestly blame yourself for an organizational problem? Did you blame yourself, or did you seek a scapegoat? If you sought a scapegoat, did you try to work out a deal with the person who took the blame, or did you simply cast off the blame on someone you didn't like or wanted to get rid of?
2. Pretend you are explaining your answer to question #1 to St. Peter, and your ability to explain it will determine the fate of your soul.
3. Describe the three most critical problems currently affecting your organization. To how many of these problems can you attach the name of a superior, inferior, or coworker? What do you believe the solution to these problems should be? If you say "fire/transfer so-and-so," are you really just passing the buck? How can you be sure that if you do get rid of these people their replacements will be any better? Are you so sure? Think again.
4. Make a list of the impairment situations you have faced in the past three months. Next to each item, list your response to it under the following headings: (a) passed the buck, (b) blamed someone else, (c) became emotional and did nothing productive, (d) took action that resulted in the resolution of the problem, or (e) did nothing and prayed the situation would somehow disappear. Now think through them again. What would you do this time if the situation reoccurred? Why?
5. Let's assume you work for a man whom you respect and admire. One day you accidentally discover he has been involved in a scheme to fraudulently channel money into his operation, some of which probably goes directly into his pocket. What do you do? Go to him, explain what you know, and leave it at that? Go to him, explain what you know, and ask for a cut of the profits? Go to him, explain what you know, and blackmail him for a promotion and raise? Go to his superior with the information, explain how you acquired it, and

hope you will be rewarded for it? Go to his superior and make a deal for the information? Do nothing, but revise your opinion of your boss? Chart the likely consequences of each one of these choices. Now what would you do?

PLAYING THE BLAME GAME

The standard reaction to trouble is to find out who was responsible. It is a peculiar belief (sort of a Freudian belief actually) that if you find the cause of a problem it will somehow repair itself. Because the problem can't be blamed, but a person can, the blame game begins. It is easy to blame someone, but blaming is a simulated activity. The blamers and the blamees look busy while they exchange insults and charges and denials, but in fact they are doing nothing to resolve the situation.

Sometimes to find out *who* was responsible is to find out *what* really happened. The supposedly responsible person may have forgotten to do something, or may have done something other than what was expected. These are human errors, and while they deserve no praise, they hardly deserve censor either. In these cases the blame game must be played with easy escape routes for the blamee. The responsible person can be located, the cause of the problem discovered, blame laid, and the situation can be corrected with the understanding it will never happen again. The key to this strategy is *neutral phrasing* when the blame is laid: "What went wrong?" rather than "You disgusting piece of cow manure, how in the hell could you forget to do something like this!!!?"

After the blamee looks sadly at his or her shoes for awhile, and shrugs, or turns beet red, or offers an apology, you need to ask the second question: "What can be done about it now?" This is the more important question because it focuses on doing something about the problem. Finding out who was responsible for it becomes incidental; finding a way out of the mess becomes the goal. Then you and the blamee can work out a solution with the understanding she or he has committed an error, as we all sometimes do.

If this strategy sounds wimpish, consider the alternatives.

You could play the "hard guy" version of the blame game, and bully the blamee into a long, pointless confession concerning his or her sins against the organization. You could threaten the blamee with loss of job, loss of face, and loss of personal pride. You could have a public fit, curse loudly and long, and say words you will later regret or wish you could take back. But these tactics usually lead to an escalation of hostilities. Do you really want to spend a considerable portion of your work days worrying about what someone you once blamed for something you've now forgotten is planning to do to you? Of course not. You want to *resolve the situation*, and to do so requires behaving in a calm, rational manner. The blamee will do more to punish himself or herself if you don't try to, then you could do if you tried. Remember the last time someone yelled at you? How did you feel? Did you feel *more* or *less* guilty for the wrong you committed? Case closed.

If the same person screws up consistently you need to provide just cause for disciplining the person, or terminating her or his employment. Most organizations have guidelines concerning how to document problems, how to process grievances, and how to handle disciplinary interviews. If you don't know what your company's policies are, find out. If your company doesn't have a clear policy, then help create one. There will always be problem people wherever you work, and instead of playing the endless, egotistical blaming game you need to find ways and means of dealing with the situations problem people create.

PREVENTIVE STRATEGIES

Of all the ships that sail across the Atlantic we remember the *Titanic*. Why? Because something went wrong. In every company there is a *Titanic* too, usually in the guise of a human being. This is the person who walks by and everyone nudges, winks, or giggles because of some catastrophic or silly event she or he was responsible for. Like Joe Bftsplk in *'Lil Abner*, this is the funny little person who walks around with a rain cloud over him or her all of the time.

We notice problems *after* they occur, and we lay blame *after* the fact. Consider this, however, before you mistakenly believe you are at the mercy of the fates and furies of organizational life: Most problems can be *prevented*, particularly those problems that affect our personal and professional reputations. In this section we want to examine some of the ways you can prevent adversity from negatively affecting you.

Protecting Your Reputation

Aristotle believed reputation was the most important element in effective performances. We agree. Of course, no one is born with a reputation. A reputation, like an education, is something you must acquire with effort. Who you are, what you know, what you stand for, and what you can persuade others to do or not to do are the foundations for a solid reputation.

Contrast reputation with fame and you have an important understanding vital to success in any organization. To be famous means to be a hero, and to be a hero means you did something right once. To have a solid reputation means you do things right most of the time. To be famous means you must inspire others by your words and deeds consistently. To have a good reputation means you lead others by your own example, only in those situations that require a leader. To be famous means to fall from grace the first time you fail to meet your audience's expectations, because nobody believes a real hero can fail. To have a good reputation means you can occasionally commit human errors without seriously damaging your standing within the organization, because the person with a solid reputation can overcome errors.

There are no corporate "Halls of Fame." For the employee of good repute an occasional note in the company newsletter is most fame she or he can hope for. But while heroes must meet steadily increasing demands on their heroism, the employee with a good reputation can choose how to make progress upward in the organization. The hero may get a large bonus once, in reward for the act of heroism; the good employee can acquire steady merit raises. And when the hero causes a catastrophe because she or he reaches too high, tries too hard, fails to meet the challenge, it is almost always the person with a good reputation who is called in to pick up the corporate pieces, and fit the puzzle together again.

So, as Aristotle knew, it is *not* fame you should be courting, but a solid reputation. For the person with respect can always try to succeed where the person with fame always risks total failure. To guard your reputation requires adhering to the following rules:

1. *Never embarrass anyone:* If someone above or below you on the organizational chart helps you, let others know about it. If someone above you behaves badly and you could embarrass him or her for the momentary pleasure a round of laughter brings, hold your tongue. Nobody forgives public embarrassment, no matter how much it is deserved. If someone below you behaves badly, call the individual into your office, take him or her into your confidence, and explain the consequences of the behavior. Then let him or her off the hook gently. You will have made an ally. If someone equal to you makes an error worthy of censor, let someone else censor her or him. No one ever acquired a good reputation by bad mouthing the competition.[5]

2. *Provide support for your ideas:* Never ask people to accept your ideas because they are *yours*. Always have good reasons to back up your claims, evidence to support your ideas. The person of good repute is a reasonable person, and reasonable people have data as well as gut instincts to guide them.[6]

3. *Admit your faults honestly:* Modesty includes the ability to admit when you are wrong. You can win respect by combining the admission of error with a plan to repair the damage. Holding fast to a bad plan, a dumb idea, or poor evidence is the sign of an egotistical fool, not a person of admirable character. As much as you believe you are right, you need to recognize that others can see when you are wrong at least as well as you can.

4. *Maintain good working relationships:* People with good reputa-

---

[5]Except presidential candidates in recent electoral history.

[6]For a practical guide to everyday reasoning, see E. P. Bettinghaus, *The Nature of Proof* (Columbus, Ohio: Bobbs-Merrill, 1979), or H. Kohane, *Logic & Contemporary Rhetoric: The Use of Reason in Everyday Life*, 3rd ed. (Belmont, CA.: Wadsworth, 1982).

tions tend to have the support of superiors, equals, and subordinates on the organizational chart. Regardless of hierarchical position, the admiration is maintained because the person with a good reputation knows how to treat everyone. These personal qualities pay off in times of crisis when you need a friend, or you need a quick way to get something done. Alienating others because you stand above them is one very good way to encourage a negative public appeal, which can ultimately damage your reputation and chances for success.

Nice guys (or gals) don't necessarily finish last, despite Lombardi's credo. Nor does the person who only looks out for Number One always succeed. There are plenty of nice persons with a genuine sense of equity who make it in any organization. Our advice is to try to be one of them. You may not get a slogan or a book named after you, but you won't die young and mean or be hated either.

Learn From Other's Mistakes

This is straightforward advice, and perhaps for this reason it is commonly overlooked. People in organizations seldom *learn* from one another's mistakes because they are too busy *dwelling* on them. Telling stories about why so-and-so got canned or punished is occasionally entertaining, but the wise person looks for the symptoms and causes of the firing, approaches the loss analytically. Unless you can find out *why* someone failed, chances are you might suffer the same fate.

You want to be known as a problem-solver, not as a problem. Past errors are an invaluable source of information about how others failed to solve problems, and can help you to solve yours. Problem-solvers are invariably rewarded. American management specialists have been looking for the secret to Japanese management success for over a decade. In one sense what seems to be the case is that in Japan, engineers account for approximately 60% of the decisions made regarding problems. In America about the same percentage of decision-makers are trained as lawyers. Where the Japanese emphasize the practical solution, the technological answer, a great many American firms emphasize arguing about who is guilty, who should take the blame, and who is "covered." The person who can stand above conflict and just get the problem solved is the truly valuable employee, and the one most likely to succeed in any organization.

Repair Style

There is some truth to the otherwise dumb dictum "Actions speak louder than words." For example, in times of crisis, talking about what you *will* do, or *plan* to do is less meaningful than actually doing something. When you are trying to solve a problem deal only with those persons who are directly involved. Explain to them what you are trying to accomplish and how you plan to do it, and tell them specifically what their role is. Above all, don't brag about the inherent goodness of your plan. When, and if the problem is solved by your actions, you can calmly point out what you *did*.

If you can identify an error and fix it before anyone notices, there is no need ever to mention it. If you are noticed while you are fixing it, it is fairly simple to be matter-of-fact about it: "I goofed but I'm taking care of it now," is a simple way of getting off the hook you would be hung on if you simply said "I goofed." It is only when you whine, refuse responsibility, try to fix blame on someone else, or make claims about what you are going to do that you get yourself into trouble.

There are some rules to follow when you have to make repairs. First, you have to admit it is broken. Problem-solving cannot begin until the problem is clearly identified. Vague feelings that something is wrong is not enough. You can't "improve morale" without first finding out what is depressing the staff. The way you *say the problem* dictates and directs what you will work on. If you say "I want to make employees feel more secure," then you are confronted with a myriad of ephemeral possibilities. If you say "I want to defuse the rumor that there are impending layoffs," you can work through the problem and hopefully resolve it.

Second, admit honestly your own role in whatever went wrong. If you were made partially responsible for the rumors because of some chance remark you made, you'll have to admit making the remark before you can do anything about the rumors. Avoid defensiveness. You can defend yourself all the way up to the end of the unemployment line. When you act defensively you usually try to pass the buck, and there are only two things that can happen when you pass the buck. You make an enemy out of the person you blame, and you begin to believe yourself. Once you begin believing yourself despite facts to the contrary, then you are behaving like Richard Nixon during Watergate. Enough said.

One additional point needs to be made about admitting your mistakes. The great American psychiatrist Harry Stack Sullivan complained about children being taught to say "I'm sorry." He argued that children who learn to say "I'm sorry" learned how to get off the hook by simply apologizing. Lessons learned early in life tend to continue into and through adulthood. Hence, there are many adults who believe all they need to do is say "I'm sorry" to get off the hook. Unfortunately, apologizing doesn't help the person you hurt nor does it correct the situation you caused. The only thing that will help is to make full restitution, to make the situation right again.

Third, you need to figure out whether it is your lack of competency, your lack of knowledge, your lack of experience, your lack of support, your lack of opportunity, your lack of time, or your lack of interest that caused the problem. Think about what you thought and what you did, not how you feel about it. If you can locate a deficiency in your actions, you can begin to correct the deficiency. If you concentrate instead on how you felt, you will inevitably only succeed in convincing yourself your feelings were justified and be none the wiser for it.

Finally, you need to correct the situation. This may translate to asking others to help you, overcoming your deficiencies, or working out the problem yourself. Whatever the corrective action needs to be, it is vital that you carry the burden of carrying it out. Others will help you if they see you taking an active role in correcting the situation you helped create, or they will think and say good things about you if they see you trying to learn from your mistakes, overcome a deficiency, or learn the necessary lesson from the experience. But as any excellent actor knows, these are judgments an audience must make based on the *actions* of the performer, not merely his or her *intentions*.

CLEARING YOUR GOOD NAME

We have provided strategies for overcoming problems and screw-ups caused by others or by you. All of these strategies assume you or someone else actually did something wrong. In this section we examine what to do if you are put on the spot for something you didn't do.

Occasionally someone may succeed in laying one on you, blaming you for something you did not do. While it is the American legal tradition that a person is innocent until proven guilty, if you try that line at the office you will find yourself the laughing stock of the organization. Everyone knows if the assumption of our legal system held true, there would have been no reason for the Miranda decision. For it is more often the case that "everything you say (and do) will be held against you." Innocence doesn't count. Your behavior in response to the charges brought against you *does*.

The first thing you have to do is figure out who blamed you and why. The best way to approach this vital issue is to ask who stands to gain if you take the blame? Among your competitors, which one may be trying to cover up something she or he did by blaming you for the problem? Among the superiors in the organization, which one fears your competency? Among inferiors, which one is slyly trying to sneak into your job? If you have evidence of duplicity or deception, there is no point to remaining silent. The time to lay blame on others with whom you work is when unjustified blame has been placed on you. And when you do lay blame on them, you had better be able to cite chapter and verse of the criminal code, dates and times of observed inefficiency or lackyism, and probable cause which would, if necessary, be able to stand up in a court of law. By the same token, if you are blamed you'd better be absolutely certain you are completely clear before you say or do anything. You can look very bad if you are accused of a crime you had a hand in committing and deny all charges, only to have it clearly demonstrated that you are both harmdoer and liar.

One of the best strategies for overcoming blame which may be partially accurate is to take your share of it and make sure the person who lays the blame on you also takes a fair share. It can be very persuasive to say "Okay, I'll take the blame for this one, even though I wasn't the only one who fouled up. But what about (fill in the name of another problem) that (fill in the name of the person who blamed you for this one) stirred up?" That puts a nice hard lob in your enemy's court, way back over the shoulder where it is most difficult to return.

If you do find yourself in a mutual blaming session, you should be fully aware of the consequences. If you lose, the only way out is out. If you win, you will have a permanent, potentially dangerous enemy. These are the hard facts of organizational life. Sometimes after a mutual bloodletting, the best thing for you to do is seek employment elsewhere, even if you won. Just make sure you do so under your own authority, and at your own convenience. Don't let it appear you were forced out. You can enjoy getting back on your feet in a new location, wiser for the experience, and cherish the trouble and troublemaker you left behind.

One final word. In the rare event that you are made the scapegoat for a major problem caused by your boss, you need to meet privately with him or her to arrange the details. The basic rule is to comply, even though it will be painful. Take the rap, cover up for the boss, save his or her tail, and be sure your payoff compensates for the misery you will experience. There is no way you can win if you beat the boss, who will, after all is said and done, still be the boss, unless of course you so thoroughly wipe out the boss that you *become* the boss.

POSTSCRIPT

You made it.

You are *there*, living the success you once only dreamed of. The performance personality you worked so hard to develop, to perfect, pays off each time you see your name in brass on the door. You have made it in America, just like you wanted to.

You feel differently about yourself. Inside you hold all the identities you have created, and most of the memories too, but there is a new sense of self that transcends mere accomplishment or pride. *You are all that you have become.* Somehow, though, it never seems to be quite enough.

Making it in any organization doesn't mean you reach a high plateau and follow it to the horizon. Nor does it mean you retire young and live out your days on the golf courses of North America. You can choose these options, of course, because you have earned the right to choose. But the performance personality will probably urge you not to. There is too much yet to be done.

One of the concommitants of making it is the need to continue making it happen. The "it" is pure emotion. It is the energy you thrive on, the sensation of being that pours through your central nervous system when you are in the thick of an assignment, on the brink of breaking the bank. It is a rhythm within you, it is a feeling. You don't ever want to let it go. Maybe you can't let it go.

You know what we mean. You have felt it, maybe only the beginnings of that marvelous emotional charge, that sense of power, calm, and control, but you have felt it. The emotion is primitive, like an instinct for survival by overcoming overwhelming odds, but it is also refined, like a highly developed sense of eloquence. It is worth having, this emotion, worth seeking after even when the seeking seems dense and endless. And so we do.

In the future is a museum in which we will be the relics, the history of things past. Our technologies and their artifacts will stand stone still in glass cases, like candies under counters from a child's eye. They will be motionless and we will be inhabitants of the gone world, the dead world, the afterlives we imagine wait for us when that last breath of polluted air passes from our lips into vast nowhere. What we leave behind will be our legacies, our gifts to those with whom we will share only a common genetic bond and the will to continue.

We think of the future like that, and immediately return to the present. The future is tomorrow, and there is still today enough for me, we say, perhaps a little less confident than we felt ourselves to be before the thought, a little less certain of what tomorrow might bring. But here we are, somewhere on the blue planet, riding the spinning orb into a destiny of our own making.

And having made it we learn only our desire can never be fully satisfied, our need for the seeking of it never fades away, and our past performances were only preludes to a sense of the present, sudden and sensuous, inducing in us the passionate will to *become*.

INDEX